The ruins of Minster Lovell Hall.

Shire County Guide 20

OXFORDSHIRE
and Oxford

Marilyn Yurdan

Shire Publications Ltd

CONTENTS

Set in 8 point Times roman and printed in Great Britain by C. I. Thomas & Sons (Haverfordwest) Ltd, Press Buildings, Merlins Bridge, Haverfordwest, Dyfed.

British Library Cataloguing in Publication Data available.

Cover: *St Helen's church, Abingdon, seen from the bridge over the Thames.*

ACKNOWLEDGEMENTS
Photographs are acknowledged as follows: Brian Archer, pages 8, 26, 37 (lower), 44, 49 (top right), 52 (top), 54, 55, 56, 57, 58, 59, 61, 62, 67; BICC, page 49 (lower); Cadbury Lamb, pages 1, 2, 3, 4, 6, 9, 11, 13, 14, 15, 21 (right), 25, 30, 32, 33, 34, 35, 37 (top), 39, 42, 47 (both), 49 (top left), 78 and front cover; Marilyn Yurdan, pages 5, 7, 16, 17 (both), 18, 19, 20, 21 (left), 23, 24, 27, 29, 31, 38, 40, 43, 45, 46, 52 (lower), 66, 68, 71, 72, 77.

Greys Court.

Culham Bridge on the Thames.

1
Oxfordshire in focus

Oxfordshire has always been a smallish county, but as diverse and interesting as any in Britain. With the county boundary changes of 1974, however, the new Oxfordshire (which now has an area of 645,000 acres, or 261,032 ha, instead of 470,000 acres, or 190,209 ha, as formerly) acquired much of scenic and historic interest from Berkshire.

As exhibits in the county's museums show, Oxfordshire has been settled since the ice age. Bones and artefacts 350,000 years old have been found in the upper Thames valley at North and South Hinksey, Kennington and Abingdon, among other places, and hunting and food gathering are known to have taken place over a large area. Neolithic sites survive, as well as many bronze and iron age ones, particularly in the Vale of White Horse, while two thoroughfares of outstanding importance to prehistoric man cross the county: the Ridgeway and the Icknield Way.

The Romans left extensive traces of their occupation, for example villas in the river valleys of north-west Oxfordshire and at Wantage, cemeteries at Wheatley and Abingdon, towns at Dorchester-on-Thames and at Alchester near Bicester, and a pottery kiln and bath-house at Headington. A major Roman road, Akeman Street, crossed the county from east to west, with minor roads leading off it.

Akeman Street was still in use in the 1540s when Leland travelled along it.

Most of Oxfordshire was settled early by Saxon tribes, who established sizeable towns here, as well as building royal manors and palaces, notably at Headington, and at Islip and Wantage, where Edward the Confessor and Alfred the Great respectively were born. Oxford's patron saint, Frideswide, was an eighth-century Saxon princess. The great majority of Oxfordshire's towns and villages were established before the Domesday survey of 1086, and many of its churches show evidence of Saxon foundation, outstanding examples being at Langford, North Leigh and St Michael at the North Gate, Oxford.

Domesday Oxfordshire, the Normans found, was very prosperous, and the newcomers built castles at Wallingford and Oxford and numerous churches, of which Iffley is the finest survivor. Many other churches have at least crypts, doorways or windows from this period. The Normans and then the Plantagenets encouraged the priories and other monastic foundations which were once so numerous, but most of them perished at the Dissolution or became domestic or collegiate buildings.

The middle ages gave Oxfordshire some of England's greatest treasures: large 'wool'

3

The battle monument at Chalgrove Field.

Cromwell was Chancellor of the university and after the Restoration Oxford became capital once again while the plague raged in London. The seventeenth and eighteenth centuries were a time of intense religious activity, when numerous nonconformist sects came into being, culminating with Methodism, born in Oxford in the 1720s.

In Stuart and Georgian times many fine manor houses and minor stately homes were built, and the enormous Blenheim Palace. Although there are few elegant Georgian crescents, much interesting domestic architecture survives in the county's market towns, and in Oxford Beaumont Buildings are tucked away behind St John Street like terraced dolls' houses.

In Victoria's reign there was little industrialisation, but a spate of building activity among the middle and upper classes. Churches were built or rebuilt by Scott and Street; nonconformist chapels were built, together with strange-looking buildings like Keble College and the University Museum. The labouring classes, however, mainly dependent on agriculture, suffered a series of economic depressions which led to considerable poverty and emigration. Some moved to Oxford suburbs like Jericho, or the near-slums of St Thomas's; others went further afield. With Cornwall, Oxfordshire sent the largest number of colonists to New Zealand. For a realistic picture of Victorian Oxfordshire Thomas Hardy's *Jude the Obscure* is probably more accurate than Matthew Arnold's 'The Scholar Gipsy', although Flora Thompson paints a more cheerful picture in *Lark Rise to Candleford*. For Oxfordshire country life in the twentieth century, Molly Harris's *A Kind of Magic* should be read.

The early twentieth century brought radical changes; the university was depopulated by the First World War, and William Morris, later Lord Nuffield, began to build those motor cars which were destined to change the face of Oxfordshire for ever.

Oxfordshire has never been heavily industrialised and so has fewer of those scars which disfigure certain other counties. Nevertheless, there has always been a wide range of industries, from the traditional to the high-technology firms which are winning awards for their exports.

Minerals extracted are iron ore in the Banbury area, sand and gravel in the river valleys, lime and cement at Chinnor and Shipton on Cherwell, and building stone at Taynton, Hornton and Headington (though stone quarrying has now virtually ceased). The county has a number of breweries (at Henley, Oxford, Hook Norton and Abingdon) and there is food processing at Witney and Banbury, with light engineering, boatbuilding,

churches and tiny country ones; glorious stonework and wonderful stained glass; valuable brasses and magnificent tombs; manor houses and country cottages, as well as many of the Oxford colleges themselves.

During the Civil War there were skirmishes at Radcot, Cropredy and Chalgrove Field, where John Hampden was fatally wounded. Several towns, including Oxford and Banbury, were besieged; Broughton Castle was a Parliamentarian stronghold, and Oxford was the Royalist capital. During the Commonwealth printing and publishing, car manufacturing, atomic energy production and tourism as well as the traditional glovemaking, blanket weaving and the educational establishments for which Oxfordshire has always been noted.

Present-day Oxfordshire stretches from the limestone and ironstone hills of the Cotswolds in the west and north-west to the chalk North Wessex Downs in the south and the chalklands of the Chilterns in the south-east. Nowhere does the land rise to any great height. To the north and west are wide plains, while the whole of Oxfordshire lies within the basin of the Thames and its tributaries.

The Downs and the Cotswolds were traditionally sheep country, and this was in part the cause of some of the deserted villages in the area, while along the river valleys the land is used as pasturage for all types of livestock. On the higher ground, for instance in the Vale of White Horse and to the north of Oxford, the farming is predominantly arable, most noticeably so on the North Oxfordshire Plain, a clay area largely devoted to the production of cereals.

The county may be conveniently divided into six regions, of which one, the city of Oxford, is largely taken up by the university and its associated buildings.

The Chilterns, with their waterless valleys, thin soil and beechwoods, are an important haunt of wildlife. The villages are brick-built, serene and mellow.

In contrast, the Cotswold settlements appear to have risen from the ground upon which they are built, so well do they blend with the surrounding countryside, and many have streams or rivers running through them. In addition to the local stone, Stonesfield slate is an attractive and much sought-after roofing material. This is wool country, the Cotswold sheep being the largest native British breed.

The Oxfordshire Plain, with Banbury as its capital, has rich reddish soil and belongs to the English Midlands rather than to Wessex, something which is reflected in the local accent. Here the stone is honey-brown rather than the grey found elsewhere in the county, and this gives the villages a warm, homely aspect.

The Thames valley, probably the best known part of Oxfordshire, has been one of England's chief thoroughfares since prehistoric times. Here are the resorts of Henley, Goring and Abingdon, the lush watermeadows of Bablockhythe and the *Wind in the Willows* country around Mapledurham. The towns and villages are urbane, polished and clearly belong to the stockbroker belt, hinting at the nearness of London.

The Vale of White Horse, one of the most remote areas of southern England, has villages in pairs, one 'East', one 'West'. This is a land of racehorses, large stretches of open downland scattered with archaeological sites, barrows, hillforts and the oldest of England's white horses cut into the chalk at Uffington. Even in the sunlight one is aware of a certain eeriness evoked by centuries of human activity.

William Morris's workshop in Longwall Street, Oxford.

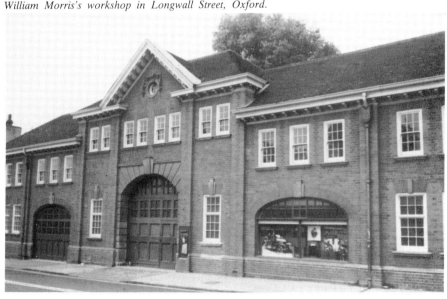

5

Aston Rowant Nature Reserve.

2
The countryside

Oxfordshire has no large areas of wild country-side, but plenty of good walking country with numerous footpaths. As elsewhere, there is a trend towards the creation of official, well signposted routes.

Oxfordshire County Council, with assistance from the Countryside Commission, has produced a series of excellent free leaflets which are available from tourist information centres and which point out items of interest for naturalists, historians and archaeologists, as well as for the layman who just wants to get away from the city and motorway.

Leaflets are also available from tourist information centres giving details and outline maps of circular 'walks from Banbury, Carterton, Eynsham, Faringdon, Oxford, Wantage and Witney. Another leaflet details farm walks from Stanton St John, on the edge of Otmoor, and there is another on the River Windrush Walk, taking in Burford, Widford, Swinbrook, Asthall and Worsham, visiting their churches en route.

Walks in the city of Oxford need not be confined to the pavement; indeed the city has the most inviting walks, the best loved being around Christ Church Meadow, in the Botanic Garden, along Addison's Walk in Magdalen College and in the University Park.

Serious naturalists should contact the Berkshire, Buckinghamshire and Oxfordshire Naturalists' Trust (BBONT) for detailed publications and information about membership and entrance to sites which are not readily accessible to the general public. The trust's address is: 3 Church Cowley Road, Oxford OX4 3JR (telephone: 0865 775476). According to BBONT, the county is 'exceptionally rich in wildlife', particularly in the Chiltern beechwoods and the Thames water-meadows. There are several secret sites where monkey and military orchids flourish, while the ghost orchid is found only in the Chilterns. Oxfordshire's main botanical speciality, though, is fritillaries. The public has free access to the BBONT reserves included in the following list.

There is a good selection of bird life, including buzzards, kingfishers and nightingales, with a heronry at Nuneham Courtenay. There are no outstanding mammals, reptiles or amphibians, but Oxfordshire is wonderful butterfly country, purple emperors, black hairstreaks and Adonis blues being noteworthy.

Historic survivals are birthwort in the ruins of Godstow nunnery, where centuries ago it was cultivated by the nuns, fat (or edible) dormice and Roman snails, both in the Cotswolds.

Aston Rowant National Nature Reserve (OS 165; SU 731966). Astride the A40 and M40, between Stokenchurch and Lewknor, and close to Beacon Hill Forest reserve and Aston Hill, which belongs to the National Trust.

The reserve consists of 104 acres (42 ha) of

chalk grassland and scrub with beechwood, on an escarpment of the Chilterns. The reserve offers good examples of chalkland fauna, and there is a nature trail.

Blenheim Park, Woodstock. ¼ mile (400 metres) west of Woodstock (see also chapter 6).

The park, apart from providing an ideal setting for Blenheim Palace and good picnicking areas, is full of ancient trees, particularly oaks. There are also deer, insects, lichens, toadstools and waterfowl on and around the lake. A nature trail booklet is on sale in Blenheim gift shops.

Chinnor Hill, Chinnor (OS 165; SP 767006). BBONT. On the Ridgeway ½ mile (800 metres) south-east of Chinnor. Access from Hill Top Lane, off the Chinnor to Bledlow Ridge road.

These 69 acres (27.9 ha) of chalk grassland are intersected by public footpaths which cross the scrubland on a Chiltern escarpment. The Icknield Way runs through the northern section. Here are juniper, frog orchids, beechwoods and fine views out over the Vale of Aylesbury.

D'Arcy Dalton Way

This long-distance footpath, opened in 1987, extends some 65 miles (104 km) and connects the Oxfordshire Way, the Thames Path and the Ridgeway. It runs from Wormleighton Reservoir, just over the Warwickshire border, to Wayland's Smithy in the south-west (chapter 3). Stiles and bridges have been built along the route and a guidebook is available from the Oxfordshire Footpath Society.

Blenheim Park, Woodstock.

Ducklington Fritillary Meadow (OS 164; SP 3607). ¼ mile (400 metres) east of Ducklington.

This fritillary meadow borders the river Windrush. It is left alone for four months of the year (March until the end of July) and then the meadow is farmed normally, but without the use of sprays or artificial fertilisers.

Horley Reserve (OS 151; SP 417434 to 407427). BBONT. ¼ mile (400 metres) south of Horley.

These 30 acres (12.1 ha) of mixed habitat have been made into an educational reserve using old ironstone workings.

Iffley Meadows, Oxford (OS 164; SP 5203). Owned by BBONT and the City of Oxford. ¼ mile (400 metres) west of Iffley.

These fine fritillary meadows are a mass of purple in the spring.

Magdalen Meadows, Magdalen College, High Street, Oxford.

These leading fritillary meadows are approached through Magdalen's main entrance, via Cloister Quad and through a doorway facing the New Building. Cross the little bridge to the right and follow the path by the Cherwell for Addison's Walk and the fritillaries.

North Leigh Common (OS 164; SP 402140). BBONT. 1 mile (1.5 km) north-east of North Leigh. Approach via A4095.

The common consists of 41 acres (16.6 ha) of heathland and scrub, with many kinds of birds, sphagnum bog and interesting flora. This is the only local site for western gorse.

7

Deer in Magdalen Grove, Oxford.

Oakley Hill, Chinnor (OS 165; SU 757995). BBONT. ¼ mile (400 metres) south of Chinnor.

The hill is 12 acres (4.8 ha) of chalk grassland and scrub.

Otmoor

Although Otmoor's 4000 acres (1619 ha) are mainly unproductive agriculturally, they are most important in that their wetlands harbour numerous species of wildlife, many of which are rare. Should the area be converted to arable farming, they would be lost to Oxfordshire. These wetlands have been called 'one of the last open wildernesses left in Britain' and their chequered pattern is supposed to have given Lewis Carroll the idea of the chess game in *Alice through the Looking Glass*. They are threatened by the Thames Water Authority's suggestion of improving the drainage of the river Ray, a waterway remarkable in that it flows backwards during heavy rain.

Otmoor is crossed by only two roads, one the Roman road running north-south from Alchester, near Bicester, to Dorchester-on-Thames. By the roadside is Joseph's Stone, believed to be a Roman milestone. The 'seven towns' of Otmoor are the small villages of Beckley, Charlton-on-Otmoor, Horton-cum-Studley, Oddington, Fencott, Murcott and Noke, and during enclosures in the nineteenth century the district became notorious for its riots and the destroying of fences. The centre of the moor is used as a rifle range and is often closed off.

In 1987 the food manufacturers Heinz gave £12,000 to help save part of Otmoor, the 56 acre (23 ha) Murcott Meadows site, just north of Horton-cum-Studley. This has been designated a site of special scientific interest by the Nature Conservancy Council and will be purchased by BBONT. It is ancient grassland where 130 plant species, of which eighteen are rare, have been discovered.

The Oxfordshire Way

The Oxfordshire Way links the Cotswolds in the west of the county to the Chilterns in the south-east and was the idea of the Oxfordshire branch of the Council for the Protection of Rural England. It runs 65 miles (104 km) from Bourton-on-the-Water, Gloucestershire, to Henley-on-Thames and is waymarked. It enters Oxfordshire near Ascott-under-Wychwood and makes its way across the county, passing near Charlbury, Stonesfield, Kirtlington, Weston-on-the-Green, Islip, Beckley, Waterperry, Rycote and Tetsworth, down to Henley in the south-east.

Pixey and Yarnton Meads (OS 164; SP 4711). ½ mile (800 metres) south-west of Yarnton.

The meads are grassland situated on both sides of the Thames. They have never been ploughed, having been managed for centuries in a traditional way.

The owners appoint two 'meadsmen', who auction the grazing and mowing rights. Origi-

8

nally the meadows were divided into sections called 'mowths', with names like 'Watery Molly' and 'William of Bladon'. After the auction lots were drawn for their distribution, using thirteen cherry-wood balls, one for each mowth. Today the rights are sold to a single taker, who is thus able to work them economically by modern farming methods. The meads are rich in flora and molluscs.

Port Meadow, Oxford. 1½ miles (2.5 km) north-west of Oxford city centre. Access from Walton Well Road, where cars may be parked. Sensible footwear recommended as the terrain is uneven and liable to flood.

Between the Thames and the railway lies Port Meadow, some 400 acres (160 ha) of meadowland which has never been ploughed throughout its long history. It is, therefore, of great interest to naturalists and historians alike, as well as to those who come here for exercise, boating or bathing.

Early inhabitants of the meadow were bronze age families; the positions of their huts can still be made out from the air. Near the north-east corner are the remains of a tumulus.

Port Meadow has belonged to the Freemen of Oxford and the Commoners of Wolvercote since Saxon days, and they are entitled to keep horses and ponies there, provided that the animals are registered. Once a year, without warning, the Sheriff, sometimes on horseback, sometimes by Land Rover, rounds them all up. This was done by helicopter on one occasion. They are released only upon payment of a statutory fee, while illegal grazers are fined £25. The horses share the meadow with geese, ducks, cows and campers.

In early July, at Wolvercote Common, the

The Ridgeway at Uffington Castle.

north end of the meadow, the Sheriff's Horse Races are held. This event goes back to the eighteenth century and is accompanied by other attractions.

Port Meadow was used as an airfield during the First World War and a plaque on the bridge at the north end commemorates two airmen who were killed nearby. Across the meadow and over the river is Medley, a favourite summer venue for trippers from Oxford at least the seventeenth century. Boats may be hired from Medley boatyard and easy walks taken either across to Binsey (chapter 5) or along the riverbank as far as Godstow, Wolvercote or Botley.

The Ridgeway

This is the seventh of the Countryside Commission's long distance paths. It follows the ancient Wessex Ridgeway and the Icknield Way through five counties from Overton Hill in Wiltshire to Ivinghoe Beacon in Buckinghamshire, a total of 85 miles (136 km), the entire length being marked with the Commission's acorn sign. The Ridgeway mostly follows the northern edge of the chalk escarpment, above the spring line, across the North Wessex Downs as far as Streatley; it then follows the east bank of the Thames, then the lower slopes of the Chilterns. The whole walk comes within areas designated as being of outstanding natural beauty.

Through Oxfordshire the Ridgeway is very rich in ancient sites (see chapter 3).

The proof that the ancient Ridgeway (the name derives from the Saxon *hrycaweg*, which was a Saxon *herepath* or war road) was a major route is provided by the stone artefacts found nearby. The raw materials of which they were fashioned came from as far away as Cornwall

and Cumbria. Tin from Cornwall, gold from Ireland and copper from Europe were taken along it, as well as cattle and warriors. It was an important artery, with plenty of look-out and defensive points, essential until the existing tribal areas were broken down by the Romans. Its use was revived in the dark and middle ages.

A Ridgeway Centre has been built at Letcombe Regis in an old chalk quarry. Five redundant barns have been turned into a hostel and visitors' centre with facilities for walkers, horse riders and cyclists. There is to be a Ridgeway display room, showing exhibits relating to the wildlife and history of the Ridgeway.

The Icknield Way, much of which now forms part of the Ridgeway path, is a 4000-year-old thoroughfare which runs from Avebury in Wiltshire to the Wash and was used by the Roman Aulus Plautius. In Oxfordshire it follows the Downs, crosses the Thames at Wallingford and winds along the foot of the Chilterns into Buckinghamshire.

A free *Ridgeway Information and Accommodation Guide* is available from tourist information centres and *Discovering the Ridgeway* by Vera Burden (Shire Publications) describes the route in detail.

Shotover Country Park and Hill, Oxford. Oxfordshire County Council. Access by minor road via New Headington, or from Wheatley.

This is the remnant of a royal forest, where John Milton's grandfather was once a ranger. The name Shotover is thought to derive from the Old English *scot ofer* or 'steep hill', although another, less likely, suggestion is *chateau vert* or 'green castle'. Today it is largely bracken-covered hillside and woodland, frequented by foxes, rabbits and courting couples. No road now crosses the plain on the top, although this was once the old London road, notorious for its highwaymen.

Shotover is built up to the west, where it overlooks Oxford, and to the east towards Wheatley, but to the north-west are Shotover House and grounds. On the outskirts of Oxford are two large areas of woodland, both of which are open to permit holders only.

Somerton Meads (OS 164; SP 492302). ¾ mile (1 km) north-west of Somerton.

This is an important wildfowl haunt, with many aquatic plants.

Swyncombe Downs (OS 164; SU 673912). 2½ miles (4 km) east of Ewelme.

This interesting Chiltern chalkland has juniper bushes and superb views over the Thames valley.

Taynton Quarry (OS 163; SP 239150). 1½ miles (2.5 km) north of Taynton.

These old limestone quarries, which provided much of the stone for medieval Oxford, are now the home of a varied flora and a good place for butterflies.

The Thames Path

Since Roman times the Thames has been a vital trade route but its importance declined with the coming of faster means of transport and the ferries which took passengers from one bank to the other stopped operating so that today's walker is sometimes left without any way of crossing the river in order to follow existing paths. The Countryside Commission is planning a continuous path along the Thames valley, from the river's source in Gloucestershire to London. The route will stay close to the river, with small diversions to nearby places of interest and it will be the first of the long-distance paths to follow the course of a river. It is also unusual in that, far from sticking to rural areas, it will link such important towns and cities as Oxford, Reading, Henley, Maidenhead, Windsor and London itself.

Warburg Reserve, Bix (OS 175; SU 720880). BBONT. 1¾ miles (3 km) north of Bix. Access by the Bix Bottom turn off A423 or from B480 at Middle Assendon.

One of the most important of Oxfordshire nature reserves, this is 253 acres (102 ha) of old-established woodland, mainly beech, with chalk grassland and scrub, crossed by public footpaths. There is an educational reserve and study area, as well as a nature trail which takes about three hours to complete. The flora is varied, consisting of some three hundred species, including seventeen species of orchids, and there are also butterflies, moths, snails, a good selection of birds, deer, badgers and foxes.

Watlington Hill and Park (OS 165; SU 702935). National Trust. 1 mile (1.5 km) south-east of Watlington.

These 150 acres (60 ha) of beechwoods and 96 acres (39 ha) of chalk grassland and scrub support many old yew trees on an escarpment of the Chilterns. There is good chalk flora, particularly mosses, as well as butterflies.

Wychwood Forest and Ponds National Nature Reserve (OS 164; SP 3316). 1 mile (1.5 km) north-east of Leafield.

The remnant of an ancient royal hunting forest which once covered a much wider area, Wychwood has fine oakwoods and limestone grassland, with varied flora and fauna. The ponds are spring-fed, and there are man-made marl ponds with crayfish.

The Rollright Stones.

3
Sites of archaeological interest

Oxfordshire is rich in archaeological sites. In Tudor and Stuart days the northern part of the county was noted for its barrows, most of them now long vanished under the plough. With the county boundary changes of 1974 Oxfordshire acquired an important range of sites previously in Berkshire, the majority in the Vale of White Horse. They date from neolithic to Saxon times.

For displays on sites in the county, with maps and articles found in them, the local museums should be visited (see chapter 7). Of particular use will be the Vale and Downland Centre at Wantage, the Ashmolean and the Museum of Oxford in Oxford, Dorchester Abbey Museum (chapter 5), the County Museum at Woodstock and Reading Museum. The Local History Collections at the Westgate Library in Oxford have a comprehensive selection of books, maps, magazines and photographs dealing with the archaeology and history of Oxfordshire and the surrounding areas.

Alfred's Castle, Ashbury (OS 174; SU 277822). Just below the Ridgeway, on the edge of Ashdown Park.

This iron age hillfort certainly pre-dates the monarch whose name it bears. Its area is little more than 2 acres (0.8 ha) and it has a single rampart and a linear ditched outwork which can be seen on aerial photographs. Although the pottery found here suggests an early iron age origin, Romano-British and Saxon pottery and metal artefacts have also been found. The name of the site may have been given in commemoration of Alfred's notable victory over the Danes near here in AD 871.

Blewburton Hill, near Blewbury (OS 174; SU 546862).

In the extreme south of Oxfordshire, between the Ridgeway and the Thames and with the Sinodun Camp hillfort to its north, the Blewburton fort is about 7 acres (2.8 ha) in area, having been enlarged from its original early iron age area of about 4 acres (1.6 ha) and surrounded by palisades. A century or two later, around 400 BC, a V-shaped ditch was made to enclose the total area, which was then defended by a box rampart. About 100 BC Blewburton was once more reinforced, only to be abandoned before the arrival of the Romans in AD 43. The ritual burial of ten horses was excavated at the entrance. The site continued to be used in the dark ages, however, and into medieval times, as proved by Saxon family burials and terraces cut into its slope.

Cherbury Camp (OS 164; SU 374963). South of the A420, near Charney Bassett.

This site was once a low-lying island,

approached from the north-east. The area has since been drained and turned into valuable farmland. The camp was excavated in 1939 and revealed an inner rampart faced with dry stone walling on both sides. Pottery, now in the Ashmolean Museum, provides evidence of occupation between the first century BC and the first AD.

Devil's Ninepins, Ipsden (OS 175; SU 633851). 1000 yards (900 metres) north of Ipsden House.

This circle of seven stones, with a flat central one resting on four others, is not an ancient monument but was built in 1827 by E. A. Reade, as a 'modern druids' temple'.

Dorchester-on-Thames Roman town (OS 174; SU 578941).

To the west of the modern village, between the High Street and Watling Lane, is the site of a small Roman walled town of about 13.6 acres (5.5 ha) which lies largely under modern Dorchester and the allotment to the west of the abbey. Visible are an earthen bank and a wide ditch-hollow to the south-west. The allotment site was excavated in 1962 and showed that it was first used in Belgic times. During the first and second centuries AD simple timber-framed houses were constructed. The eastern rampart round the town dates from the late second century AD, and the stone wall in front of it is a century later. The town was still in existence in the early fifth century, possibly housing a Roman garrison, but it seems likely that within the next fifty years it was taken over by Saxons who, contrary to form, built among the Roman ruins. In the Abbey Museum (chapter 5) are photographs and plans which explain the archaeology of the Dorchester area in detail.

Grim's Ditches

There are at least three separate earthworks in Oxfordshire bearing the name 'Grim's Ditch', which is thought to come from the Saxon 'Grim', or Devil.

One exists just below the Ridgeway and runs parallel to it between Wantage and the A34 (SU 423845 to 542833). Its purpose may have been to prevent livestock from wandering off the Downs and becoming lost in the forested areas of the Vale.

A second Grim's Ditch is found in north-west Oxfordshire, mainly in Spelsbury parish, where it runs through Ditchley Park, and appears again west of the A34 above Over Kiddington (where there is a Grimsdyke Farm) and Old Woodstock. It is in a series of lengths, never continuous, and is thought to have been constructed in the first century BC by the Belgae. It is clearly visible in Blenheim Park (OS 164; SP 427183) and south of

Charlbury (OS 164; SP 360185).

A third Grim's Ditch is at Mongewell, near Crowmarsh (OS 175; SU 608883 to 682868). This linear earthwork, which probably dates from the first century BC, runs from the Thames to the top of the Chiltern Hills, a distance of about 5 miles (8 km). The dyke faces south, to stand as a barrier between the river valley and the hills. It is crossed by the Icknield Way south of Blenheim Farm and gives a good walk of about 3 miles (4.8 km) between the A4074 and Nuffield village.

The Hoar Stone, Enstone (OS 164; SP 378236). Near the crossroads on the B4022, south-west of the A34.

In a small walled enclosure stand the remains of a ruined megalithic tomb consisting of six stones. Three are standing and three lie on the ground in front of the tomb. In 1824 a mound about 39 inches (1 metre) high stood here but it has now disappeared.

A single standing stone is the **Hawk Stone** at Chadlington (OS 164; SP 339235), which stands on a ridge to the east of a road which connects Dean and the B4026. It is 8 feet (2.5 metres) high and is near a possible Danish encampment.

A third single stone is the **Thor Stone** at Taston, near Spelsbury, which takes its name from the stone (OS 164: SP 360222). This great stone, 6 feet (1.8 metres) high, and in its natural state, is named after the Norse god of thunder.

Hoar Stone Long Barrow, Steeple Aston (OS 164; SP 458241).

In a wood along a bridlepath between Barton Abbey and Rousham Gap stands a long mound 49.9 feet (15.2 metres) long with a heap of broken sandstones at its east end. The barrow was destroyed in 1843 but its stones were collected and piled up on the site. It might once have been a cairn with either a terminal burial chamber or a false entrance.

Lyneham Camp Hillfort and Long Cairn, Lyneham (OS 164; hillfort SP 299214, cairn SP 297211).

Beside the A361, on a southwest-facing hill slope, this small circular camp encloses 6.4 acres (2.6 ha) and has a single rampart and ditch. Excavations showed a rampart, still 5.9 feet (1.8 metres) high, stone-faced both inside and out. There was a U-shaped ditch, 6.9 feet (2.1 metres) deep and 18 feet (5.5 metres) wide. A gap in the rampart to the north was the original entrance. Lyneham Camp is more likely to have been a cattle pound than a defence work.

To the west of the A361, some yards north of the camp, is a neolithic long cairn, about 164 feet (50 metres) long, overgrown and

12

ruinous. On the barrow is a standing stone 5.9 by 4.9 feet (1.8 by 1.5 metres) and 18 inches (46 cm) thick. The barrow was opened in 1894, when a ridge of very large stones was noted running along its spine. Two rectangular burial chambers were found to the south-east, and human and animal bones scattered throughout the mound. Two Saxon graves were found on the site, but the whole has been severely damaged by ploughing.

North Leigh Roman villa, North Leigh. Telephone: 0993 881830. English Heritage. Between the hamlet of East End and Combe, 4 miles (6 km) south-east of Charlbury. At East End, go past the Leather Bottel, take the lane to the right, and the villa is at the bottom of the field to the right. The lane is too narrow for cars to turn round to come back.

One of nearly a dozen Romano-British farms and country houses in the lower Glyme and Evenlode valleys, where they are crossed by Akeman Street, this villa was one of the most sophisticated. The home of a middle-class Romano-British family, it was started in the first or early second century AD. Like the one at Ditchley, this villa would have originally consisted of the dwelling house, an outhouse and a bath-house. Over the next century or so its owners extended it considerably until by the fourth century it had become a very desirable residence with more than sixty rooms. These were arranged round a courtyard and had three sets of baths with hot and cold water, mosaic pavements and underfloor heating in some rooms. The villa seems to have suffered a serious fire and to have been abandoned quite soon after it reached its full size. Edible snails, introduced by the Romans, can still be found in the vicinity of North Leigh.

The Rollright Stones, near Chipping Norton (OS 151; King's Stone and King's Men SP 299308, Whispering Knights SP 296308). On a minor road connecting the A34 and A44, north-west of Chipping Norton.

These prehistoric megaliths were famous throughout all England in the middle ages. They have suffered from weathering and from mutilation by the local peasantry who would chip off pieces to carry as talismans. The Rollright Stones are arranged in two groups, not all of which are considered to be contemporary. The larger group forms a circle some 100 feet (30.5 metres) across and includes some 77 stones (though they are said to be uncountable), which vary from a few inches to 7 feet (2.2 metres) in height. Their inner surfaces are flatter than the outer ones, as if they have been hand-worked but show no trace of tool marks. The circle probably dates from the bronze age. About 100 yards (91 metres) to the north, across the road, is the 8 foot (2.5 metre) high solitary King Stone, which has suffered badly from the attentions of the superstitious. It stands on a low mound, which is not a long barrow as has been suggested.

About 400 yards (366 metres) east of the circle are four upright stones in a group about 5½ feet (1.7 metres) square, with a fifth stone, originally placed on top of the others. This second group is known as the Whispering Knights and is thought to have been a neolithic barrow.

The Rollright Stones are only a part of the rich selection of barrows that once existed in the vicinity. According to legend, the Stones represent a king and his army who had come to conquer England. As they marched uphill, a witch suddenly barred their way, just as the king was about to reach the top of the hill. From there he should have seen the Warwickshire village of Long Compton. The witch cried out that if he could indeed see this village he would become king of England. He was

Sinodun Camp is an iron age hillfort on the Wittenham Clumps.

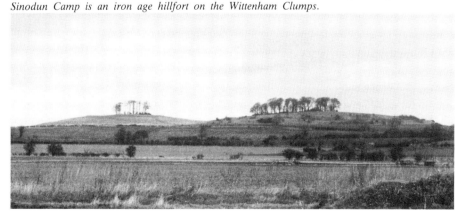

delighted and took seven strides forward, but when he reached the top he found a long mound of earth in front of him. The witch told him that as Long Compton was not visible he would not become king of England and, furthermore, he and his army would be turned into stones. The king became petrified near the mound, his soldiers in a circle behind him, and the witch herself turned into an elder tree. The smaller group of stones, the Whispering Knights, were traitors who lagged behind the main army in order to plot against their king.

Segsbury Camp, Letcombe Regis (OS 174; SU 385845). On Segsbury Down, to the north of the Ridgeway.

Also known as Letcombe Castle, the camp comprises just over 26 acres (10.5 ha) within a single ditch and a rampart once faced with sarsen stones. These stones were frequently carried off by local people for building material. The original entrance is to the east, but the rampart is broken where a road passes through running north to south. Finds at Segsbury include a hoard of Roman coins and a stone presumed to be a Roman altar. West of the village of Letcombe Bassett is a deep natural hollow known as the Devil's Punch Bowl.

Wayland's Smithy.

Sinodun Camp, Little Wittenham (OS 164; SU 570924).

The camp, set on a steep hillside, affords sweeping views over the Thames. It is kidney-shaped and approximately 10 acres (4 ha) in area, enclosed by a deep ditch, the material from which went to build its outer rampart. Iron age pottery from the camp is to be seen in local museums.

Uffington Castle, Uffington (OS 174; SU 299864). National Trust.

The castle is situated 856 feet (261 metres) above sea level, on a peak of the chalk escarpment, and has views over the Vale of White Horse towards the Thames. It covers an area of 8 acres (3.2 ha) and is oval, with a rampart and ditch to defend it. The entrance is to the west. Some excavation was done in the nineteenth century, but the castle remains relatively undisturbed. Iron age pottery found here indicates occupation from about 500 to 300 BC by hill farmers. Uffington Castle features in many old photographs as a favourite destination for outings in Victorian and Edwardian days. While the National Trust is carrying out important restoration work entry to certain sections of the castle is restricted.

Wayland's Smithy, Ashbury (OS 174; SU 218854). Off a short track north of the Ridgeway.

Overlooking the Vale of White Horse, this large chambered long barrow was constructed by an early farming community and is the burial place of several generations. Radio-carbon dating has established that it was built between 3700 and 3400 BC.

The Smithy consists of a facade of sarsen stones, some over 10 feet (3.1 metres) high and weighing 4 tons, with a cross-shaped burial chamber inside. Excavations in 1919 and 1962/3, when the Smithy was restored, showed that the monument was constructed at two different periods. First, a wooden chamber with a stone floor was built, and here were found the bones of at least fourteen skeletons. The bodies had been in varying stages of decay when put there, probably because it was the practice to expose bodies to the elements before the actual burial. When the chamber was full, sarsen stones and chalk from two side ditches were placed over it in a mound about 6 feet (1.8 metres) high, 54 feet (16.5 metres) long and 27 feet (8.2 metres) wide.

Later a long mound was built over the first barrow, with two stone-lined chambers leading off an entrance passage. This second mound was 180 feet (54.8 metres) long, with a width varying between 48 and 20 feet (14.6 and 6.1 metres), being wider at the south end. In its chambers were eight skeletons. When the

Above Uffington White Horse.

burying finished, the chambers were filled in with rubble; then the barrow and the adjacent farmland were abandoned.

It seems that the name Wayland's Smithy is Saxon, as a charter of AD 955 mentions 'Weyland's Smithan'. Weland was a character in north European mythology who learned the smith's trade from trolls. The story of a mysterious smith is told in Sir Walter Scott's *Kenilworth:* if a traveller tethered his horse near the Smithy and left a coin on the capstone, Weland would shoe the horse overnight.

The White Horse, Uffington (OS 174; SU 301866). A few hundred yards north of the Ridgeway, at Uffington.

The horse, after which the Vale and an Oxfordshire district are named, is the oldest of the fifteen horses cut into the chalk downlands of England. It is probably also the most famous, being mentioned in Thomas Hughes's books *Tom Brown's Schooldays* and *The Scouring of the White Horse.* Its origins remain uncertain. Some experts claim that it is iron age because of a marked similarity to a horse found on coins of that period, but others say it is Saxon. Its most probable use was to mark either a tribal boundary or a meeting place. There is no proof that it was cut to commemorate Alfred's victory over the Danes at the battle of Ashdown in AD 871, the battlefield itself being unidentified. The first written reference to the horse is in an eleventh-century document from Abingdon Abbey and by the fourteenth century it was considered a major attraction second only to Stonehenge.

The horse measures approximately 360 feet (111 metres) long and 130 feet (40 metres) tall. It is little more than an elongated outline, at no point more than 10 feet (3 metres) tall. The periodic scourings to prevent the grass from obscuring it, combined with erosion, have gradually altered its shape. In Georgian and Victorian days scourings were accompanied by picnics, games and competitions. It is still considered lucky to stand on the horse's eye and make a wish.

Below the horse is a depression called the Manger, and nearby is Dragon Hill, where traditionally St George slew his monster, proof being offered by the fact that the patch where grass refuses to grow has been poisoned by a trickle of dragon blood.

Widford church (OS 163; SP 271121). ½ mile (800 metres) west of Swinbrook.

Widford is almost a deserted village, with little more than its church and one old house. Services in St Oswald's church ceased in 1860 and by the beginning of the twentieth century it was badly decayed. During restoration in 1904 a Roman pavement was discovered.

St Oswald's is very simple, with no tower or aisle. There is much Norman work and a font believed to be Saxon. The most interesting feature, however, is the Roman pavement, two sections of which are on view at the west end of the chancel. From the design, they would seem to date from the mid fourth century AD. The church was probably designed to stand on this Roman site and Roman objects have frequently been unearthed during gravedigging. It is not known what kind of building the Roman structure was.

Today the church is in excellent condition and services are held during the spring and summer. Visitors should also note the church's wall paintings. There is a large St Christopher opposite the main door and a hunting scene portraying the Three Kings Living meeting the Three Kings Dead in a forest and reminding them of their fate.

Pre-Reformation Oxford with Osney Abbey church in the foreground.

4
Castles and monastic ruins

In the century after the Norman conquest of 1066 much monastic building took place in the Oxford area as well as the construction of **Beaumont Palace** for the king at the west end of today's Beaumont Street (only a doorway now remains). Over the following centuries other foundations appeared, doubtless attracted by the royal palace and the growing influence of the university.

Some important religious houses have now vanished but played a considerable part in the history of pre-Reformation Oxford. **Osney Abbey** was founded in 1130 for Austin Canons by Robert D'Oilley II. The abbey had an enormous and imposing church, as is shown in a window in the cathedral commemorating Robert King, last Abbot of Osney and first Bishop of Oxford. Osney Abbey occupied a site now covered by the cemetery and some side streets to the south of the railway station. **Rewley Abbey** was a Cistercian house founded by Edmund, Earl of Cornwall, on a site to the south-west of Beaumont Palace, where Rewley Road is now. Most of its remains were removed when a coal wharf was constructed, leaving only a fifteenth-century doorway near Hythe Bridge.

At **Littlemore** a small Benedictine nunnery was founded in the mid twelfth century by the lord of Sandford-on-Thames. The site is now covered by farm buildings, some of the nunnery's stones being incorporated into the farmhouse. Near **Sandford** church is the site of a manor house given to the Knights Templar by the Sandford family. Today there is a Tudor farmhouse, and a large barn where their church once stood.

In the Museum of Oxford (chapter 7) is an artist's impression of medieval Oxford, its monastic buildings, halls and hostels dominated by the massive church of Osney Abbey. Remnants of religious foundations were bought up and incorporated into various colleges at the Dissolution, for example at Worcester, Trinity and Christ Church.

Abingdon Abbey, 18 Thames Street, Abingdon.

This Benedictine abbey was founded in 690, twice sacked by Danes and finally completed about 1170. Its royal apartments were used by several monarchs and by the fifteenth century it was second in England only to Glastonbury. The abbey was suppressed in 1538 and demolished. Its stone was sold until only a handful of buildings was left. In 1945 these were bought and restored by the Friends of Abingdon and are now open to the public.

The Entrance Office is part of a building of the twelfth to thirteenth centuries; probably originally a barn, it became a bakehouse and then a prison. It houses pictures and maps of the abbey. The fine thirteenth-century Chimney forms part of the Checker and has a vent below from the Undercroft fireplace. The Checker Hall, now the Unicorn Theatre, has a good fifteenth-century roof. It has been altered considerably and became a house. The Checker itself is late thirteenth-century, with a noteworthy fireplace. Its name implies that it was the abbey exchequer, or treasurers' room. The Long Gallery, early sixteenth-century, was probably used as a dormitory and divided up into several rooms leading off an open corridor. On a roof truss are traces of paintings. The Lower Hall, once a brewery store, was originally similar to the Long Gallery above. The nineteenth-century Cosener's House over the mill stream derives its name from the abbey kitchener's house which stood here. The Undercroft, a stone-vaulted chamber, has a central pier, fireplace and blocked doorway. The church site is marked by crosses where successive high altars stood; the ruins are a nineteenth-century folly. St Nicolas's church, just outside the abbey precincts, was used by its lay servants and tenants. Under the nave runs a culvert carrying the river Stert, which marks the parish's western boundary; thus the tower and rest of the nave are in the next parish!

Deddington Castle, Deddington.

Approached from the Market Place and Aynho Road, massive grass ramparts are all that remain of the Norman castle at Deddington. The Castle Grounds are now a large recreation field. In Deddington Castle Edward

Right: *Abingdon Abbey: the Chimney and the Unicorn Theatre.*

Below: *Remains of Beaumont Palace, Oxford, the birthplace of Richard Coeur de Lion.*

II's favourite Piers Gaveston was incarcerated before he was taken to be hanged on Blacklow Hill, outside Coventry, in 1312. Castle Farm, by the square, is a sixteenth-century stone house with balustrades and parapets. It contains much stone from the castle, and Charles I slept there after the battle of Edgehill in 1642.

Godstow Nunnery, Oxford. To the north-west of Oxford, reached through the village of Wolvercote, at the far end of Port Meadow.

Godstow Nunnery was a community of Benedictine nuns living on a site on the west bank of the Thames given by a lord of Stanton

17

St John. It was consecrated in 1138 in the presence of King Stephen and his queen. Legend tells that Henry II's mistress, Fair Rosamund Clifford, repented of her immoral life and retired to Godstow. Another version says that she was killed by Henry's jealous queen, but it is certain that Rosamund was buried here in 1177 and that her tomb became something of a shrine. In 1191 Bishop Hugh of Lincoln, while visiting Godstow, was disgusted to find a royal concubine in such a tomb and ordered her immediate removal from the nunnery church. Eventually her bones were placed in a perfumed leather bag, enclosed in lead and replaced in the church.

The nunnery was suppressed at the Reformation and became a private house, which in turn was destroyed in the Civil War. All that now remains is part of the enclosing nunnery walls and the ruins of a small chapel, where a ghostly mass was reported in the 1970s.

Hanwell Castle, Hanwell. South of the minor road which links the A41 and the A423 north-west of Banbury.

This massive brick tower with stone quoins and large mullioned windows, which are blocked up, dates from the sixteenth century and bears a similarity to contemporary buildings such as Hampton Court and the gatehouses of some Cambridge colleges. Hanwell Castle formerly had four such towers, one at each of its corners, but this is the lone survivor. The castle was built by William Cope, 'cofferer to the household' of Henry VIII, and was the home of the Cope family for about three hundred years. In the 1780s a destructive owner tore down the main building leaving only the one tower and a few adjacent buildings, which in time became a farmhouse.

To the east of the castle were terraced gardens and fishponds, but only one pond survived into the twentieth century.

Minster Lovell Hall, Minster Lovell. Telephone: 0993 75315. English Heritage.

The ancient village of Minster Lovell has a fifteenth-century bridge over the Windrush, a lovely old church of the same age, the well known Old Swan Hotel and Minster Lovell Hall, a fifteenth-century house built round a courtyard.

Its ruins stand in low-lying meadowland near the Windrush and were once the home of the Lovel family. Constructed in the 1430s, the house remains sufficiently intact for it to give a fair impression of its original layout. The principal surviving sections are the walls of part of the north and west sides of the court, and the hall, complete with fine windows and carved, hooded fireplaces.

Francis, ninth Lord Lovel, was a favourite of Richard III and known as 'Lovel the Dog' from his emblem. After Richard's death in 1485 at Bosworth Field, Lovel escaped but two years later again took up arms against Henry VII at the battle of Stoke. Once more he fled the battlefield. Some say he escaped to France, but locally it is believed that he came back to Minster Lovell, where he hid away in a secret locked room, known only to one trusted retainer. When something happened to this servant, Lovel probably died of starvation. In 1708, during alterations, a human skeleton was found, seated at a table, with paper and pen in front of it and a dog's skeleton at its feet. This macabre tableau was 'so much mouldered' that it fell to dust.

A similar legend, also connected with the hall and several other old houses, is that of the

Ruins of the chapel and enclosing wall of Godstow Nunnery.

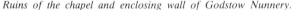

Mistletoe Bough, in which a bride played hide-and-seek on her wedding night, locked herself into a wooden trunk and was unable to escape; her skeleton was not found until generations later.

Minster Lovell Hall was dismantled in the 1740s and used as farm buildings until its restoration in the 1930s by the Ministry of Works. A short walk away is a well restored fifteenth-century dovecote, circular and with hundreds of pigeon holes. The birds provided a valuable source of fresh meat for the household during the winter.

Oxford Castle, Oxford. A few hundred yards from the Westgate Centre, down Tidmarsh Lane, within the precincts of Oxford Prison.

Only the tower and crypt of the church of St George in the Castle and the castle mound remain and may be viewed either from the road or nearby footpaths. Visits, however, may be arranged with an authorised member of the Oxford Guild of Guides (details from the Information Centre in St Aldates).

In 1071 Robert D'Oilley, Governor of Oxford, built a large, well defended castle to the west of the existing Saxon city. Its main entrance was in what is now Castle Street, behind the County Hall. A model of this Norman structure, made by prison inmates, is on view in the Museum of Oxford.

During the winter of 1142 Queen Matilda was besieged in Oxford Castle by her cousin and rival for the throne, Stephen. Dressed entirely in white, she escaped over the snowy field and made her way along the frozen Thames to the safety of Wallingford Castle.

Oxford Castle gradually decayed, although it was used as a prison and the assizes were held there until 1577, when a horrific outbreak of jail-fever killed about three hundred people and caused that session to become known as the Black Assize. After this courts were held in the Town Hall until the present County Hall was built in the nineteenth century on part of the castle site.

Official visitors may descend a stone staircase into a well chamber dating from the twelfth or thirteenth century and peer down a shaft 54 feet (16.5 metres) deep, in which several skeletons were found during excavations. There is a view from the top of the mound over south and west Oxford, Boars Hill, Cumnor and Wytham, and northwards to Walton Street and the Radcliffe Observatory in Green College.

Wallingford Castle, Wallingford. Entrance in Castle Street, up a turning behind the George Hotel.

The castle site is designated an ancient monument; part of the grounds has been laid out as very pleasant public gardens, with

The tower of Oxford Castle.

lawns, shrubs, benches and a fountain. There are a few remaining ramparts, some stonework and ditches, one of which runs north, south and west, another east by the Thames. To the north is the town ditch, while the motte at the south end of the inner bailey has traces of masonry. To the east is an early fourteenth-century window and, to the south-west, stonework from St Nicholas's collegiate church; this is early sixteenth-century and incorporates a window.

These items are the sole remains of Wallingford's once proud castle, built by Robert D'Oilley in 1071. It was the refuge of Matilda in 1142 after her flight from Oxford, the scene of the signing of the Treaty of Wallingford which brought an end to the civil war in 1154, and the gift of Henry V to his bride, Catherine de Valois, in 1420. Chaucer's son, Thomas, was constable here, but in the sixteenth century the castle declined and much of its stone was taken to Windsor to repair the castle there. Wallingford was strong enough, however, to withstand a Parliamentarian siege for 65 days. The town was the last one in England to hold out for Charles I; Cromwell remembered this and later ordered the castle to be demolished.

As the paths are made of flints and fairly steep, visitors are advised to wear strong shoes.

19

The effigy of Sir John Holcombe in Dorchester Abbey.

5
Churches and chapels

Oxfordshire has a fine small cathedral and hundreds of churches and chapels of architectural and historical interest, the majority containing treasures and curiosities. The county is particularly rich in brasses and medieval wall paintings. As befits the cradle of Methodism, there are several examples of early nonconformist chapels, for example Cote Baptist church near Witney. The Oxford college chapels are dealt with under the colleges in chapter 10. Inclusion in this book does not imply that these churches are always open; fortunately many parishes deposit keys in nearby houses or shops, while others operate a 'church watch' scheme.

Abingdon: St Helen.
The original thirteenth-century church was remodelled in the fifteenth and sixteenth centuries, the result being today's large and attractive building with its impressive range of aisles and chapels. The inner north aisle forms the Lady Chapel and has an amazing late fourteenth-century roof, with a Jesse tree, although the figure of Jesse has perished. The chapel was built by William Reeve and re-paired in 1935. The outer north or Jesus Aisle has a Victorian white marble font displayed at the Great Exhibition of 1851; it is a copy of the one at Sutton Courtenay and has a cover dated 1634. Here also are the sixteenth-century tomb of John Roysse, founder of Abingdon School, and two ancient bibles. The inner south or St Katherine's Aisle has several brasses, and the outer aisle, dedicated to the Holy Cross, is dated 1539. In the nave, or St Helen's Aisle, are the pulpit (1636) and the seventeenth-century carved mayor's seat.

Adderbury: St Mary.
St Mary's was started in the thirteenth century and enlarged in the next. Its octagonal tower and spire are a landmark. Outside, above the east window, are the arms of William of Wykeham, founder of Winchester College and New College, Oxford. The manor of Adderbury once belonged to the see of Winchester, and Wykeham's arms appear again on chancel roof corbels. Adderbury is noted for its fine fourteenth-century carving, executed by an artist who also worked at Bloxham and other neighbouring churches. In the early fifteenth century a magnificent chantry and vestry were added, both by Richard Winchcombe. St Mary's underwent extremely sympathetic restoration in the 1830s, using techniques borrowed from the fifteenth century. Further restoration by Scott in the 1860s was inspired by fourteenth-century craftsmanship at Bloxham.

Binsey: St Margaret of Antioch.

Approached from Oxford via Binsey Lane, off Botley Road (or by foot across Port Meadow), this tiny church lies about half a mile (800 metres) north-west of Binsey village. It consists of porch, chancel, nave and belfry and is said to occupy the site of an eighth-century church founded by St Frideswide, who fled here to escape the attentions of Prince Algar. The chancel has a thirteenth-century piscina. The font is tub-shaped and inside the pulpit is a carving of Frideswide by Eric Gill. The painted royal arms are those of Queen Anne.

In the churchyard is St Margaret's Well, said to have sprung up in answer to St Frideswide's prayers. It is referred to in *Alice in Wonderland* as Binsey 'treacle mines', Lewis Carroll's version of a local joke, 'treacle' deriving from *theriaca,* Latin for 'antidote', because the well's water is said to cure eye disorders.

Bladon: St Martin.

The original medieval church was the mother church of Woodstock 2 miles (3 km) to the north. By 1804 it had become so decayed that the present church was built by order of the Duke of Marlborough. It has fine views across to Blenheim Park from its west door.

The graves of the Churchill family are in the churchyard near the tower. They include the simple grave of Lord Randolph Churchill and that of Sir Winston, who chose to be buried here rather than in London. After his funeral in 1965 his body was brought by special train to Hanborough station and then on to St Martin's, where his plain white gravestone is often decorated with flowers from admirers. Around him lie several generations of Churchills.

Burford: St John the Baptist.

At the bottom of the High Street is Burford's great wool church, a Norman foundation with various aisles and chapels added over the centuries by wealthy wool merchants. The decorated west doorway is Norman, as is the base of the tower. In the north aisle St Peter's Chantry, which was used as a pew by the owners of Burford Priory, has a tall wooden canopy and screen. The bowl-shaped Norman font was re-cut in the fourteenth century and has 'Anthony Sedley Prisner' scratched into its lead lining. Sedley was a Leveller imprisoned here by Cromwell. The pulpit was remade in 1878 from medieval wood panels. The tombs of many benefactors have been spoiled and their brasses stolen but several fine table tombs remain, notably those to the Sylvester family (1568 to 1626). An outstanding tomb commemorates Sir Lawrence Tanfield (1625), his wife, their daughter and their grandson, Lucius Cary, second Lord Falkland, and his wife, all with figure-head effigies. Below the tomb a skeleton lies on a mattress.

In the churchyard are bale tombs representing woolpacks, a Roman stone coffin and the grave of the novelist J. Meade Faulkener. Here also lies Christopher Kempster, Wren's

Below left: *The Churchill graves in Bladon churchyard.*
Below right: *The church of St Andrew, Chinnor.*

21

clerk of the works for St Paul's Cathedral. Bullet marks in the church wall are reputed to be from the execution of three Leveller leaders in 1649, the scapegoats of four hundred mutineers imprisoned here. There is a plaque to their memory.

Chinnor: St Andrew.
Set below the ridge of the Chilterns, the church's exterior is mostly fourteenth-century, the tower having a low, gabled roof. St Andrew's has medieval tiles and several oil paintings, possibly by Thornhill. The altarpiece is 'The Entombment', in the style of Titian. Memorials include a fourteenth-century knight, probably a Danvers. Chinnor's collection of brasses is one of the largest in England. The majority represent fourteenth-century knights, priests and civilians. St Andrew's also has important mid fourteenth-century stained glass in its chancel and north aisle.

Cogges: St Mary.
The church and vicarage were once part of the late eleventh-century Cogges Priory, a small two-celled building. North and south aisles were added and, under the eastern half of the chancel, a crypt. About 1340 a finely carved north chapel was added, and the north aisle was rebuilt with an unusual diagonal tower which is square at the base, octagonal further up and a pyramid at the top. The mid fourteenth-century chest tomb is that of Isabelle de Grey, and on the Blake Memorial are William (1695), Sarah (1701) and Francis (1681), the men very flamboyant with enormous wigs, cravats and brocade coats.

Dorchester-on-Thames: Abbey Church.
An Anglo-Saxon cathedral founded by Bishop Birinus in 635 was superseded about 1140 by an abbey church of Augustinian canons. Over the next two centuries it was greatly extended and today is over 200 feet (61 metres) long, with a squat turreted tower and eight bells dating from the fourteenth century.
The church contains some of the earliest glass left in England, dating from the late twelfth century. It was made in France and the Rhineland and forms mosaic-like pictures. The early sixteenth-century Jesse window in the north wall of the sanctuary shows Jesse lying on the window sill, while from his body emerges a stone and glass family tree tracing Christ's descent from Jesse, and spreading across the whole window. Although Christ and the Virgin and Child have been smashed, it is the only survivor of its kind in England today.
The Lady Chapel has a very rare statue of a crusader, Sir John Holcombe; killed in 1280 in the Second Crusade, he lies here frozen in the act of drawing his sword. Nearby is the

modern shrine (1964) of St Birinus, incorporating parts of its fourteenth-century predecessor. By the pulpit is the brass of Abbot Beauforest, who in 1536 bought the dissolved abbey church for the town at a cost of £140. In a glass case is a cope described as seventeenth-century, but almost certainly earlier.
Near the entrance is the excellent Norman lead font, and in front of it is a slab to the memory of Sarah Fletcher, who died 'of excessive Sensibility' in 1799 (see Clifton Hampden, chapter 12).
Dorchester Abbey Museum, in the former monastery guest-house, consists of an exhibition of objects and displays about the area from prehistoric times. The Old Grammar School, endowed in 1652, was once housed in this building. The guest-house dates from the fourteenth and fifteenth centuries. The south side is of stone, the north of brick and timber-framed, with an overhanging first storey.

Ewelme: St Mary.
The church was started about 1430 when Geoffrey Chaucer's granddaughter, Alice, married William de la Pole, Duke of Suffolk. An earlier church was dedicated to All Saints. St Mary's was completed in mid century and is uniform in style. Its brick battlements with squared stones and flints are unusual in Oxfordshire and reminiscent of East Anglian churches. The octagonal stone font, topped by a wooden cover 10½ feet (3.2 metres) tall and crowned by a figure of St Michael, was a gift from the couple's son, Duke John. The St John's or Hospital Chapel has an open timber roof with carved angels, six of them modern. The east window glass shows the arms of de la Pole, Neville and Chaucer. The altar is modern, by Ninian Comper.
Duchess Alice's tomb (about 1475) is a masterpiece. She wears a coronet and, on her left arm, the Garter, most unusual on a woman; it served as an example to Queen Victoria of the correct way to wear it. Alice lies on the stone chest which contains her remains, but below she is represented as a cadaver in her shroud. Nearby is the altar tomb of Thomas Chaucer (1434), Alice's father and son of Geoffrey, with his wife, Matilda. Their tomb is adorned with a wonderful display of shields of families connected with the Chaucers.

Forest Hill: St Nicholas.
The church has a Norman chancel arch but no aisles. It was remodelled in the thirteenth and nineteenth centuries, and its large bellcote is clearly visible from the A40. Over the south door is an Early English porch with an ancient mass dial. Inside is a twelfth-century piscina and a seventeenth-century text is painted over

22

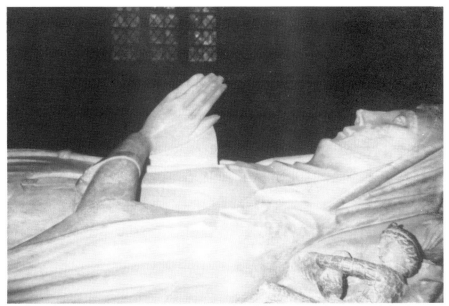

Ewelme church: the effigy of Alice, Duchess of Suffolk, wearing the Order of the Garter.

the chancel arch. Although the nave roof is dated 1630, it is chiefly nineteenth-century.

Forest Hill has some special fifteenth-century embroidery. On reddish brown velvet, it shows flowers and biblical creatures. Originally a cope, it has been cut down into an altar frontal. It is of first-class workmanship and in excellent condition.

In 1643 John Milton, 31 years old, married a local girl, seventeen-year-old Mary Powell, in the church. This totally unsuitable marriage ended in bitterness and the poet's pamphlet on divorce.

Great Milton: St Mary.

A Norman foundation clearly showing workmanship of all the great architectural styles, St Mary's was much restored in the middle of the nineteenth century. The porch, with a stair turret leading to a room above, and the chancel tiles are fourteenth-century. Below the tower is squeezed a fine seventeenth-century alabaster tomb of the Dormer family. Behind Sir Michael, his wife and his father, Sir Ambrose, hang a funeral helm and sword. Other memorials include two late thirteenth-century carved crosses. An alcove contains a broken acoustic jar which would resonate and thus improve the efforts of the choir.

Great Milton's most unusual possession is a medieval portable altar, rediscovered in 1850. Made of greenish brown marble, it is set in the main altar and has five consecration crosses. It would have been taken to the homes of parishioners too sick to attend church.

Hatford: St George.

The Norman church of St George was mentioned in Domesday Book in 1086 and retains some Norman work, although it has lost its small tower. There is a late thirteenth-century effigy of a man holding a heart. This isolated spot was the scene of the wedding in 1555 of the daughter of the Duke of Somerset, Lord Protector during Edward VI's minority, to Edward Umpton, a local gentleman. By the end of the nineteenth century St George's was so decayed that another church, Holy Trinity, was built in 1873/4 but the new church was declared redundant in 1972 and sold. St George's, its chancel roof repaired, is now back in regular use.

Horley: St Etheldreda.

This small village north-west of Banbury has a late Norman church with much medieval work, while major alterations and additions took place in 1320. The pulpit (1836) was decorated with pictures from the life of Ethel-dreda in 1950. In the north aisle is an enormous fifteenth-century painting, 8 by 12 feet (2.4 by 3.6 metres), of St Christopher carrying the Christ child over a river. The figures converse in 'bubbles'. Horley has other paintings: a small one on a pillar believed to be either St Etheldreda or St Osyth, and fifteen

23

mysterious roundels on another pillar. Ring-shaped, each contains a small letter 't' and four small solid circles. Arranged in five rows of three, they are fourteenth-century, all in crude red-ochre paint. They may represent anchors or fish hooks or be a tally.

Hornton: St John the Baptist.

Hornton stone was used for Liverpool Cathedral but its own parish church dates from the twelfth century. Like its neighbour Horley, Hornton has wall paintings, the most important of which are late fourteenth-century. Over the chancel arch is a Last Judgement, with the dead rising from their graves, and a central Crucifixion shows Our Lady and St John. Near the arch are a pietà and St George and the Dragon. More fragments are in the south aisle. In the north aisle are seventeenth-century texts and the Prince of Wales's feathers.

Iffley: St Mary the Virgin.

The church was built by the St Remy family in 1170 and is one of the most important Norman parish churches in England. The original church, built on the remains of a Saxon one, consisted of chancel, tower and nave, perhaps with an apse to the east of today's choir. Modernisation took place between the twelfth and sixteenth centuries, with sympathetic modern restoration. The exterior is most impressive with three highly decorated Norman doorways. The south doorway shows

Iffley church, showing the Norman doorway.

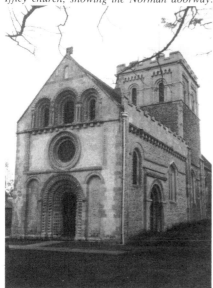

symbols of good, to the right, and evil, to the left, including Henry II. The carving is incomplete, indicating that it was executed *in situ*. A blocked-up arch is either a priest's door into an apse or a window on to the altar for the use of Annora, a thirteenth-century anchoress. This arch and a small window in the east gable may be Saxon.

The font, large enough for the total immersion of an infant, is made of black stone, with three spiral columns and one plain one. On the north wall of the sanctuary is a round *Agnus Dei*, probably the head of the churchyard cross. Four of the original twelve consecrational crosses survive on the walls of the tower and nave; unfortunately three are partially covered. The pulpit (1907) is by Ninian Comper. The entire Romanesque west window and its surround were inserted in 1858 to replace a fifteenth-century usurper of the original Eye of God window. Medieval glass fragments include the arms of John de la Pole, Duke of Suffolk.

Langford: St Matthew.

St Matthew's has very important Saxon work in its central tower and south porch but they may date from after the Norman Conquest, considering their high quality and Langford's appearance in Domesday Book as a royal manor. The parapet of the rubble tower was added about 1200 and there is a good Saxon sundial. In the thirteenth century aisles were added and the chancel was rebuilt and enlarged. An unusual thirteenth-century aumbry has three gables and six divisions. An inscription of 1691 to the Howse family tells us that 'Within this little howse three Howses lie'. Further examples of Saxon work are two sculptured crucifixions. One, on the gable end of the south porch, has been tampered with so that St John and Our Lady face away from the cross and Christ's arms are in the wrong position. The second, the famous Langford Rood, is on the east wall of the porch and shows a headless Christ triumphant.

North Leigh: St Mary.

The Saxon tower dates from the first half of the eleventh century and has Norman battlements. Set into the modern south porch is a Norman doorway but the rest of the fabric is late medieval, restored and added to in the nineteenth century. The glorious Wilcote Chapel has beautiful fan vaulting and was designed as a place of prayer for the souls of Dame Elizabeth Wilcote, her two husbands and her sons. On an alabaster tomb Sir William Wilcote is portrayed in Lancastrian armour, while Elizabeth wears a jewelled headband and hairnet. Both Wilcotes wear the Lancastrian SS collar. Here too are the parents of Speaker Lenthall of Burford.

Langford Rood.

The second north aisle was built by Christopher Kempster in the seventeenth century. A fifteenth-century wall painting of a Doom has been under whitewash and restored. The righteous are welcomed into Heaven by St Peter, but the wicked, including a bishop, wait at the mouth of Hell. Before the high altar are medieval curtain rings from which a curtain would have hung to hide the altar during Lent in pre-Reformation days. North Leigh also owns an unusual collection of coffin plates.

Oxford: Carfax Tower.

Before it was demolished in the nineteenth century, St Martin's church stood at Carfax crossroads in the centre of Oxford. The tower and a gateway leading to the former churchyard are all that remain. It was once the city church, where townspeople would gather in times of danger, triumph or disaster. Once the tower was higher than it is today, but the citizens were ordered to remove the top section in case they threw missiles on to gownsmen below. Every quarter of an hour the quarter-boys, known as Gog and Magog, strike their bells. It is permitted to climb Carfax Tower for a small fee.

Oxford: Cathedral Church of Christ.

Christ Church (as it is always known) is England's smallest cathedral and it is the only college chapel to have cathedral status.

Until 1525 an Augustinian monastery, St Frideswide's Priory, founded in the eighth century by Oxford's patron saint, occupied the site. The earliest surviving buildings, however,

date from the twelfth and thirteenth centuries. These are the cathedral itself, part of the cloisters and the chapter house (1225), which has fine bosses and corbels and roof paintings. The chapter house displays church plate and houses the cathedral shop. In the slype an audio-visual show runs, then one enters the cathedral by the south door, with its Faith, Hope and Charity Window (1871, William Morris).

In the south transept are monuments to cavaliers who died in Oxford during the Civil War; three of them were the king's cousins. The flags belong to the Oxfordshire and Buckinghamshire Regiment, with the Garter Banner of Prince Paul of Yugoslavia nearby. The tomb of Robert King (died 1557), last Abbot of Osney and first Bishop of Oxford, has a window above it showing King with Osney Abbey in the background.

In St Lucy's Chapel is the wonderful Becket Window (1320) commemorating the murder of the saint in 1170. Becket's head was replaced by plain glass by order of Henry VIII but was restored in the twentieth century. The choir is part of the original twelfth-century church, with side chapels added; it was stone-vaulted in 1500 by William Orchard and is an outstanding example of Perpendicular workmanship. The nave was shortened by Wolsey and has carved capitals similar to those at Canterbury.

In the Lady Chapel are the remains of St Frideswide's shrine. Built in 1289, destroyed under Henry VIII and rebuilt from surviving fragments in the nineteenth century, it has very early examples of carved botanical speci-

The tower of St Martin's, Carfax, Oxford.

(1297), brought here from Osney Abbey. In the eastern or St Frideswide's Window (Burne-Jones, 1858) is shown the life of the saint, ending with her death and translation into heaven. At the west end of the north aisle is van Linge's Jonah Window, complete with gourd tree but without the whale.

The cathedral spire dates from the early thirteenth century and is one of the earliest in England.

Oxford: City Church of St Michael at the North Gate.

The North Gate was demolished in 1772 but the mid eleventh-century tower of St Michael's survives in Cornmarket. This Saxon tower is Oxford's oldest building and probably formed part of the city's fortifications. It may be climbed for a fee and there are 97 steps divided into levels. First comes the library, then the treasury with an eleventh-century sheela-na-gig or fertility symbol. On the staircase is the cell door where the Martyrs were imprisoned; next are the clock room and the belfries, and finally the roof, from which there is a view over central Oxford.

The main part of the fabric is medieval and Shakespeare stood by the fourteenth-century font (which came from St Martin's, Carfax, when it was demolished in 1895) when he was godfather to the son of the landlord of the Crown in Cornmarket. John Wesley preached from the fifteenth-century pulpit in 1726. The church has Oxford's oldest stained glass, which dates from the thirteenth century. The Lily Window, showing Christ rising from a lily, is of the fifteenth or early sixteenth century.

The ancient custom of beating the bounds (parish boundaries) takes place on Ascension Day.

Oxford: St Mary Magdalen.

'St Mary Mag's', opposite the Randolph Hotel, is of Norman origin but the oldest existing parts date from the thirteenth century. The church is unusual in that it is as wide as it is long, with nave, aisles and chancel. The Victorian north aisle is known as the Martyrs' Aisle and, like the adjacent Martyrs' Memorial, commemorates the deaths at the stake of Protestant martyrs in 1555/6. This aisle, by Scott, is significant because it is the first authentic neo-Gothic work undertaken in Oxford. The interior, with statues and candles, gives the impression of a Catholic rather than an Anglican church. St Mary's has a chest of around 1300, and its fourteenth-century font is highly decorated. The glass includes scenes from the history of the church and the city. In the east window is Mary Magdalen herself.

Oxford: St Mary the Virgin.

The university church in the High Street

mens. The saint's body was removed in Tudor times and reburied in an unknown grave, although an inscription marks the reputed site. The late fifteenth-century wooden watching loft, or chantry, was installed to guard the shrine but was not used after the Reformation. Also in the Lady Chapel are the fourteenth-century tombs of Lady Elizabeth Montacute (1354), granddaughter of Simon de Montfort, of a prior (1316) and of Sir John Nowers (1386) lying under a large alabaster effigy.

In the Latin Chapel (about 1330) services were held in Latin until 1861. Nearby is the gravestone of Ela, Countess of Warwick dates from the late thirteenth century, the main part of its fabric being late fifteenth-century. The northern section, Congregation House, is early fourteenth-century and was the first university (as opposed to college) building. In 1320 a library room, the forerunner of the Bodleian, was added over the top of it.

Inside St Mary's, under the gallery, is the Vice-Chancellor's massive chair, used during university sermons. Here lie Amy Robsart (1560), the ill fated wife of Elizabeth I's favourite Leicester, and Adam de Broome, vicar of St Mary's and founder of Oriel College. Another vicar, John Henry Newman, later converted to Catholicism and became a cardinal. Latimer, Ridley and Cranmer were tried at St Mary's before they were burnt at the stake.

For a fee one may climb a narrow spiral staircase up the church tower, and on the first floor is Oxford Brass Rubbing Centre (chapter 8). In summer a film, *The Oxford Experience,* is shown in Congregation House, while concerts are held throughout the year in the church itself.

Oxford: St Peter in the East.
St Peter's is no longer a church but the library of St Edmund Hall. Visitors are admitted to the Norman crypt, dating from about 1130, on application to the college lodge, but not to the main building. The nave, chancel and the remains of a large round font are also Norman. The north chapel is said to be the Lady Chapel which St Edmund of Abingdon built with the proceeds of his lectures. In the peaceful and well kept churchyard lies the Stuart antiquary Thomas Hearne and there is a stone commemorating England's first aeronaut, James Sadler, a pastry cook who in 1784 made a hot-air balloon and travelled 5 miles (8 km) in it.

South Leigh: St James.
South Leigh's Norman chancel was virtually rebuilt in 1871 during restoration; its pulpit was used by Wesley after his narrow escape from drowning at Swinford. Near the south door is a large fifteenth-century wall painting showing a soul being weighed by St Michael. Opposite is a devil, weighing it down and summoning assistance on a trumpet. Luckily the Virgin is putting her rosary on the soul's side. There is a Last Judgement over the chancel arch, while the Virgin appears in another wall painting in the chancel, and St Clement is one in the nave aisle. From the mouth of a decayed sea monster sprouts a tree with seven dragons, each representing a deadly sin and with a human in its mouth. A seventeenth-century oil painting shows the Assumption of the Virgin, and a rare medieval metal Christ Crucified is set into a processional cross. The figure was buried at the Reformation and dug up in a garden in 1860.

South Newington: St Peter ad Vincula.
The fabric of St Peter's dates from the twelfth century to the fifteenth and there is a twelfth-century font. The parish owns an outstanding collection of 894 burial-in-wool affidavits, some with skeletons and other symbols of human mortality. These date from the period when the law required the dead to be buried in woollen shrouds.

There are some extremely fine wall paintings executed in oils on plaster. They are: a Last Judgement (fourteenth-century); St Margaret and a dragon; the Passion (late fifteenth-century), simple and archaic; St James and the painting's donor; the Virgin and Child (fourteenth-century), together with the donors, Thomas and Margaret Gifford; the Martyrdom of Becket; and the execution of Thomas, Earl of Lancaster, in 1322.

Sparsholt: the Holy Rood.
The church is large for this tiny village in the Downs. Its earliest fabric is late twelfth-century and includes the north doorway with its original iron scrolls. The chalk-built chancel is early fourteenth-century and has an Easter sepulchre, sedilia and piscina.

Sparsholt has three fourteenth-century effigies of the Archard family: Sir Robert (1353) and his two wives. These are rare, not only

The rebuilt shrine of St Frideswide in Oxford Cathedral.

27

because of their giant size but also because they are made of oak. Only 96 wooden figures survive in England and Wales and it is remarkable to find three together. They are hollow and would once have been painted and gilded. Other monuments include a brass to a dwarf of the Fettiplace family.

In the chancel is cut a plan for nine men's morris, a simplified version of draughts which is mentioned in *A Midsummer Night's Dream*.

Spelsbury: All Saints.
The church has a massive restored Norman tower which once had a spire. The entire fabric was restored in 1740 by the Lord Lichfield who built nearby Ditchley House. In two windows and on the ceiling are the arms of Beauchamp, Earls of Warwick. Two of Spelsbury's best known burials are now unmarked, those of Henry, Lord Wilmot (1657), and his son, John, Earl of Rochester (1680), the Restoration poet.

From Civil War days are the tombs of Sir Henry Lee, ancestor of the American general, and Sir Edward Lee, first Earl of Lichfield, with an imposing wall monument. He married a daughter of Charles II and Barbara Castlemaine. The third Earl has a grey and gold monument with a coffin, a snake and a cherub tying an inscription to a tree. More human is the inscription to George Pickering, a servant to the Lees for thirty years, who died in 1645. He is represented as 'creeping neere their tombes adored side, to show his body, not his duty dyde'. In the churchyard is a brick-lined rectangle containing human bones, presumably a sort of charnel.

Stanford-in-the-Vale: St Denys.
This largish church dates from the late twelfth century. Its bells came from St Peter in the East, Oxford, in 1970. The south porch was built in 1472 to celebrate the marriage of Anne Neville, daughter of Warwick the 'Kingmaker', to Richard of Gloucester, later Richard III. A Stanford girl, Jane Colyns, was nursemaid to their son.

In the chancel is a piscina with a shelf above which is a carved pyx canopy, supposed to have once held the finger of St Denys. In the churchyard is a stone carved with a frying pan in memory of a gipsy woman who died while cooking. There is also a memorial to Captain Hatt, High Sheriff of Berkshire, who fought at Culloden.

Thame: St Mary the Virgin.
The present building was constructed about 1230-40 under the auspices of Robert Grosseteste, Bishop of Lincoln. It is cruciform with nave, transepts and a central tower. Changes and extensions continued until the Reformation, and the windows show an almost complete range of styles. The chief monuments are those of the Quatremain and Williams families. In the south transept lie Thomas Quatremain (1342), his wife Katherine and son Thomas (1396), with his wife Joan, all portrayed in brass. Nearby are Sybil and Richard Quatremain (1478); Richard was councillor to Richard, Duke of York, and Edward IV and was builder of Rycote Chapel (chapter 8). A smaller brass is to Richard Fowler, possibly a godson. The magnificent black and white tomb of Lord Williams (1559) and his wife has lovely alabaster figures, and there are brasses to Geoffrey Dormer (1502), with his two wives and 25 children, and to Richard Boucher (1627), who taught John Hampden here.

In the churchyard is a good assortment of gravestones.

Waterperry: St Mary.
The oddly shaped roofs and wooden west tower give St Mary's a rather higgledy-piggledy appearance. The church contains Saxon and Norman work, the thirteenth-century chancel being on the site of a Saxon apse. There are still box pews, complete with old candlesticks, for there is no electricity. The faded arms of George II appear and the three-decker pulpit dates from 1632. Robert Fitz-Elys, lord of the manor, lies here in mid fourteenth-century plate armour, beautiful and accurate in detail.

Waterperry's chief treasures are its grisaille (uncoloured) glass of about 1220, north of the chancel, and its palimpsest brass. This brass first commemorated two fifteenth-century Londoners, Simon and Mrs Kamp. It was later re-cut and new heads and shoulders were drawn for Walter and Isobel Curzon in 1527, in Austin Friars' church, Oxford. The shoes were also re-designed, from the medieval pointed toes to the Tudor squared ones. At the Dissolution the brass was moved to Waterperry, where Curzon had been a manor tenant.

Witney: St Mary the Virgin.
Almost certainly a Saxon church stood here. Of the Norman one only a little remains, the fabric being mainly Early English. Witney's thirteenth-century spire rises 150 feet (46 metres) from the massive tower and the chimes of the clock (1876) play hymn tunes.

A door leads to a small room over the porch, formerly the home of a chantry priest. There are several small chapels built by wealthy merchants, such as the Wenmans whose altar tomb was removed from their chapel in 1867. It has a brass to Richard (1501), his two wives and children. The fourteenth-century Wenman Chapel, once used as a schoolroom and now a meeting room, has a monument to the family and an ogee aumbry.

Thame church.

Other features of St Mary's are a sundial, Norman zigzag work in the organ chamber and several other aumbries.

Yarnton: St Bartholomew.

The first church recorded here was in 1160, when the living belonged to Eynsham Abbey, but there are no easily identifiable remains. Near the south porch is a fourteenth-century cross, probably donated by the abbey. When the Spencer family moved to Yarnton in the late sixteenth century the church was in a bad condition, so the family repaired it and built the tower, with its ring of bells, and the Spencer Aisle. Then an oak screen was added, thus making the aisle into a chapel. This houses tombs of the Spencers, the older effigies being brightly painted. There is heraldic glass showing their genealogy, and on the ceiling nearly five hundred gold stars on a blue background.

After nearly a century of decline William Fletcher, an Oxford draper, undertook major restoration at his own expense in 1793. This included the installation of fifteenth-century oak pew-ends, a fifteenth-century font from St Michael's at the North Gate, Oxford, and wonderful stained glass. Fletcher lies here in a table tomb which he designed himself containing a medieval stone coffin from Godstow Nunnery. There is a portrait brass and an epitaph written by Fletcher himself. In the chancel are four carved alabaster panels, showing the life of Christ. They were unearthed from beneath an old house in Oxford.

Milton Manor House.

6
Historic houses and gardens

Oxfordshire's historic houses range from the stately Blenheim Palace to small family-run manor houses, some of which are open to the public on only one or two occasions a year, usually for charity. Intending visitors are advised to enquire about opening dates and times well in advance or to watch the local press for details. The following houses are open to the public regularly.

Ardington House, Ardington, Wantage OX12 8QA. Telephone: 0235 833244. South of A417, 2½ miles (4 km) east of Wantage.

Built in 1719 by the Strong family, master masons, Ardington House was commissioned by Edward Clarke. As one of the Strongs had recently been working on Blenheim Palace under Vanbrugh, a considerable amount of experience must have been brought to Ardington. The main feature is the two spectacular staircases, one each side of the hall, which combine into one halfway up. It is the only staircase of its kind in Britain.

Ashdown House, Ashbury. Telephone enquiries: 0494 28051. National Trust. 2¼ miles (3.5 km) south of Ashbury on B4000.

The house was built in the second half of the seventeenth century by the first Lord Craven. Pevsner described it as the 'perfect doll's house'. It is four storeys high, constructed of blocks of chalk, with a mansard roof crowned with a cupola and gold ball. It is all in the Dutch style and was built for Elizabeth of Bohemia but she died before she could settle there.

The deer park was enclosed by the monks of Glastonbury Abbey during the middle ages. It is a large oval enclosure and originally had an internal ditch with ramparts and a paling on the top.

In the fields in front of Ashdown House are some sarsen stones, known as 'Merlin's sheep' or the 'grey wethers'. There are similar stones at Avebury and Stonehenge.

Blenheim Palace, Woodstock, Oxford OX7 1PX. Telephone: 0993 811325.

Blenheim (pronounced 'Blennum'), the home of the Dukes of Marlborough, is one of England's most stately homes and was the birthplace of Sir Winston Churchill. Built for the first Duke, John Churchill, the hero of the battle of Blenheim (1704) and other major victories over the French, the palace was given in thanks by a grateful nation, its site being the ancient manor of Woodstock, favoured by the Plantagenet kings. The palace was designed by Sir John Vanbrugh and contains a magnificent collection of tapestries, sculpture, furniture and paintings in its gilded state rooms. One of its main features is the Long Library of ten thousand volumes, another the family chapel. There is also a Churchill exhibition which includes the room Sir Winston was born in.

The palace itself, the Italian garden, the French water terraces, the pleasure grounds and cascade and an arboretum are set in over 2000 acres (809 ha) of parkland, landscaped by 'Capability' Brown. One may pay for entry to the park only and wander there at will, visiting Fair Rosamund's Well, the lake, which was constructed by damming the river Glyme, and the Column of Victory. Other attractions at Blenheim include an adventure play area, a butterfly house, a narrow-gauge railway and a motor launch. Blenheim Park is also an important wildlife site (see chapter 2).

Broughton Castle, Broughton, Banbury OX15 5EB. Telephone: 0295 62624. 2½ miles (4 km) west of Banbury on B4035.

Broughton Castle stands on an island within its own moat, surrounded by a park. It has been the home of the Lord Saye and Sele and his ancestors since the fourteenth century. Internally, the castle is preserved as a family home with fine panelling and fireplaces, period furniture and plaster ceilings. The highlight of a tour of the castle is the oak drawing room with its wonderful interior porch and superb panelling. The original house, which dates from 1300, survives to a large extent, with later additions from between 1550 and 1600. Historically, the castle is noteworthy because of its involvement in the Civil War, when secret meetings of leading Parliamentarians took place there. The eighth Lord Saye and Sele was host to many of the most prominent men of his day and by his discreet, sometimes devious behaviour earned the nickname 'Old Subtlety'.

Buscot Park, Faringdon. Telephone: 0367 20786. National Trust. Between Lechlade and Faringdon on the A417.

This beautifully restored eighteenth-century house is the home of the Faringdon Collection, which includes Regency furnishings, wall paintings by Burne-Jones, much beautiful furniture and many paintings including both old and new masters. In the park are water gardens and many interesting trees.

Also at Buscot, and owned by the National Trust, is **Buscot Old Parsonage,** an early eighteenth-century house in 10 acres (4 ha) of ground.

Chastleton House, Moreton-in-Marsh. Telephone: 060874 355. Off the A44 Moreton-in-Marsh to Chipping Norton road.

Chastleton House was built for Walter Jones, a wealthy Witney wool merchant, in 1603, on an estate formerly owned by Robert Catesby of Gunpowder Plot notoriety. It bears a passing resemblance to Hardwick Hall in Derbyshire, with its imposing three-storey frontage and towers at each end but, once inside, the visitor is made to feel as if in a private home. Chastleton is noted for its Jacobean plasterwork, its panelling and carved fireplaces, as well as the long gallery which runs the whole length of the rear of the house and is decorated with daisies, roses and fleurs-de-lis. It also has a secret room, hidden just off the main bedroom, where the Royalist Jones successfully hid from his Roundhead enemies.

The gardens were designed to be in keeping with the period of the house. Opposite, in a field, stands an eighteenth-century dovecote.

Greys Court, Rotherfield Greys, Henley-on-Thames. Telephone: 04917 529. National Trust.

This sixteenth-century home of the Knollys family incorporates a fourteenth-century great tower. Today it is a mellow country house, furnished in sympathy with its age and history. Like Minster Lovell Hall, Greys Court is associated with the legend of the Mistletoe Bough (chapter 4). It is surrounded by gardens and parkland, which include the Archbishop's

Blenheim Palace.

31

Maze, of Christian significance. The National Trust also owns the lordship of the manor of Rotherfield Greys, with 25 acres (10 ha) of common land, including Greys Green and Shepherds Green.

Kelmscott Manor, Kelmscot, Lechlade. Society of Antiquaries. South of B4449 between Bampton and Lechlade.

Away from the village of Kelmscot, down a lane by the Thames, is the grey stone Elizabethan manor, which dates from about 1570. In 1871 it was rented by the Pre-Raphaelite William Morris, who used it as a country home until his death in 1896, although he never owned it. He is buried in the churchyard. In Morris's book *News from Nowhere* (1892) there is a woodcut showing the house and a description of it. Morris's daughter lived at the manor until 1938. The Pre-Raphaelite decor is still intact. The house was restored in 1963-6 and is open by appointment only.

Kingston House, Kingston Bagpuize, Abingdon OX13 5AX. Telephone: 0865 820259.

The owner, Lady Tweedsmuir, and her husband, assisted by their family and friends, show visitors round this lovely manor house. It was built in the reign of Charles II, probably by Sir Roger Pratt, a pupil of Inigo Jones, and is notable for its panelled rooms and the cantilevered staircase.

The gardens include some seventeenth-century stable buildings, a Georgian gazebo

built above an Elizabethan cockpit, and a woodland garden. They are surrounded by parkland and nearby is the small parish church.

Kingstone Lisle Park, Kingstone Lisle, Wantage OX12 9QG. Telephone: 036782 223. South of the A417 Faringdon to Wantage road.

The park is situated at the foot of White Horse Hill, near the Blowing Stone. The house was built in 1677, with two later wings added between 1812 and 1820. It houses a collection of seventeenth-century glass, needlework, carpets and furniture.

The tour includes the hall and staircase, the morning, sitting, dining and drawing rooms and the billiard room, which contains a collection of letters written by Lord Raglan, commander-in-chief in the Crimean War and great-grandfather of the owner, Mrs Leopold Lonsdale. The house's main feature is its lovely 'flying' staircase. Nearby is the village with its twelfth-century church.

Mapledurham House, Mapledurham, Reading RG4 7TR. Telephone: 0734 723350. Signposted off the A4074 Reading to Oxford road.

This Elizabethan mansion beside the Thames was built by Sir Michael Blount in 1588, the year of the Spanish Armada; it is lived in today by descendants of the Blount family. Alexander Pope was a frequent visitor, and Mapledurham is said to have inspired

Chastleton House.

32

The water garden at Buscot Park.

Kenneth Grahame's Toad Hall. The red brick, made into patterns, gives the exterior a pleasantly rosy aspect. Inside there are paintings and family portraits dating from the sixteenth century as well as a Strawberry Hill Gothick family chapel, oaken staircases and plasterwork ceilings. In the entrance hall is a collection of wooden animal heads of the seventeenth and eighteenth centuries.

A restored fifteenth-century watermill at Mapledurham is the only working corn and grist mill on the Thames. Wheat is ground using the original mechanism and millstones, and the flour is on sale in the mill and gift shop. A mill at Mapledurham is mentioned in Domesday Book.

Mapledurham village has early seventeenth-century almshouses and a late fourteenth-century church with monuments to the Blount and Bardolph families. The living is in the possession of Eton College. The Roman Catholic south aisle remains in the ownership of the family. The church has an unusual arcaded oak ceiling.

Milton Manor House, Milton, Abingdon OX14 4EN. Telephone: 0235 831287. On a minor road between Drayton and Milton.

Originally a small seventeenth-century manor house, Milton Manor was converted into an eighteenth-century gentleman's residence by the architect Stephen Wright, for George III's lacemaker, Bryant Barrett, whose descendant

still lives there. The manor has welcomed many important guests, principally William of Orange, who heard the news of James II's flight during his stay, and Tsar Peter the Great, who visited Admiral Benbow at Milton when on his way to Oxford to receive an honorary degree. The most important architectural feature of the manor is its Strawberry Hill Gothick library and chapel.

Nuffield Place, Nuffield. Telephone: 0491 641224. 7 miles (11 km) north-west of Henley-on-Thames, off A423.

The home of William Morris, Lord Nuffield, from 1933 to 1963, Nuffield Place was built in 1914 and enlarged by Morris in 1933. Some rooms remain in 1930s style as furnished by Lord and Lady Nuffield. The contents include clocks, rugs, tapestries and 1930s furniture made by Cecil A. Halliday. The house is surrounded by gardens laid out about the time of the First World War, complete with mature trees and stone walls.

Pusey House Gardens, Pusey, Faringdon SN7 8QB. Telephone: 036787 222. ½ mile (800 metres) south of A420, 12 miles (17 km) west of Oxford.

These fine gardens include herbaceous borders, rose gardens, a lake and water garden, a plant centre and many fine trees. The house is not open to the public.

Rousham House, Steeple Aston OX5 3QX. Telephone: 0869 47110. West of A423, south of B4030, 1 mile (1.6 km) south of Steeple Aston.

A late example of the work of William Kent who remodelled the house in 1738, Rousham was built originally for Sir Robert Dormer in 1635. It was later enlarged by William St Aubyn in 1860. Most of the original interior was left intact by Kent, and there is panelling from the seventeenth century, contemporary staircases and furniture, and paintings and bronzes collected over the years. The exterior resembles a Tudor mansion. Built in the Gothick style, it is reached through a courtyard, passing on the way a stable block crowned by a wooden clock-tower.

The gardens remain virtually as they were when first laid out by Kent and are rightly famous. There are cascades and ponds (in Venus's Vale), a cold bath, a portico, a temple of the mill, waterways and various other 'classical' attractions. The church dates from about 1200.

Stanton Harcourt Manor, Stanton Harcourt, Oxford OX8 1RJ. Telephone: 0865 881928.

Stanton Harcourt, a small village of thatched cottages, with a medieval church and the ancestral home of the Harcourt family, stands in open meadowland near the Thames. The church is of Norman origin and has monuments to the Harcourts, notably Robert, standard-bearer to Henry VII at the battle of Bosworth Field in 1485; the remains of his flag hang above his tomb. A Harcourt lady wears the Garter insignia: the only other known example of a woman doing so is at Ewelme (see chapter 5).

Not much remains of the Harcourts' old seat, deserted for Cokethorpe Park in Queen Anne's reign; later they moved again, to Nuneham Courtenay (chapter 12). Their Stanton home fell into disrepair and was largely demolished in 1755: only the domestic chapel with its tower above, the gatehouse and the Great Kitchen remain. The tower is known as Pope's Tower because the poet Alexander Pope had been loaned the use of the rooms by the Harcourt family in 1717 and 1718 in order to work on his translation of the *Iliad* there. He scratched on a window pane: 'In the year 1718 I Alexander Pope finished here the fifth volume of Homer.'

The Great Kitchen is the earliest part of the original house and dates from about 1380. The building is unique in England and possibly Europe; the only building resembling it in design is the Abbot's Kitchen at Glastonbury, Somerset, which is considerably later in date. In the garden can be seen the remains of the manorial fish and stew ponds.

The manor house complex provides a good example of medieval domestic architecture.

The gatehouse, facing on to the street, is early sixteenth-century, with Victorian and modern additions and is the home of Mr and the Honourable Mrs Gascoigne, she being the

Pusey House Gardens.

34

Stonor Park.

daughter of the late Lord Harcourt.

At the other end of the village stands Parsonage House, known locally as the Pest House because the fellows of All Souls' College retreated here during times of plague.

Stonor Park, Stonor, Henley-on-Thames RG9 6HF. Telephone: 049163 587. Off the B480 Henley to Watlington road.

Stonor Park is the home of Lord and Lady Camoys and has been in the Stonor family for more than eight hundred years. Stonor is situated in the Chiltern Hills and is surrounded by a deer park. The house was built near the site of a prehistoric stone circle, which has been reconstructed within the grounds. The house contains rare furniture, paintings and drawings, together with tapestries and sculpture.

As befits the home of one of Britain's premier Roman Catholic families, Stonor's chapel is used for the celebration of the mass,

as it has been since the middle ages. There is an exhibition illustrating the life and works of St Edmund Campion, who found sanctuary there in 1581, and a display of model soldiers staged by the British Model Soldier Society.

Studley Priory Hotel, Horton cum Studley, Oxford. Telephone: 086735 203 or 254. North-west of Oxford, off the B4027 Wheatley to Islip road.

As its name suggests, the Priory Hotel stands on the site of a twelfth-century priory. At the Dissolution it was bought by John Croke, in whose family it remained for over three hundred years, the west range having been converted into an Elizabethan manor house. The hotel was used in the film *A Man for All Seasons,* the story of St Thomas More. Although one of Oxfordshire's leading hotels, Studley Priory welcomes visitors (not just guests) who are interested in the history and architecture of the building.

7
Museums

Oxfordshire has a very extensive range of museums, from the world-famous Ashmolean to smaller and more intimate ones which show the past life in many of the county's towns and villages. A third type is the specialised museum, while yet another kind is the working museum, of which Oxfordshire has several examples. Intending visitors are advised to find out the opening times before making a special journey.

ABINGDON
Abingdon Museum, County Hall, Abingdon. Telephone: 0235 23703.

Occupying the top storey of the old County Hall (1678), the museum has a comprehensive collection of items tracing the history and archaeology of the Abingdon area. Highlights include displays on Abingdon Abbey (chapter 4), the borough's pewter plate and specimens of buns thrown during Abingdon's bun-throwing ceremonies, which date from 1887. These take place at times of national rejoicing, such as royal weddings.

BANBURY
Banbury Museum, 8 Horsefair, Banbury OX16 0AA. Telephone: 0295 59855.

The museum uses the word 'Banburyshire' to describe the area which it covers. It is concerned mainly with trade and industry from the Banbury area and there is a display on the vanished Banbury Castle. The museum also houses a photographers' gallery and work by local artists.

BENSON
Benson Veteran Cycle Museum, 61 Brook Street, Benson OX9 6LH. Telephone: 0491 38414. Open by appointment only.

This privately owned museum owns 450 old bicycles from the period 1810 to 1930.

BLOXHAM
Bloxham Village Museum, The Court House, Bloxham, Banbury. Telephone: 0295 720283.

The old Court House belongs to the Bloxham Feoffees, trustees of the charities of this lovely north Oxfordshire village. Its contents show aspects of life in bygone Bloxham, one of the most interesting villages in the area.

BURFORD
Tolsey Museum, High Street, Burford. Telephone (secretary): 036781 294.

The museum is situated in the ancient toll-house of Burford and shows the social and economic history of this famous Cotswold town.

CHARLBURY
Charlbury Museum, Market Street, Charlbury. Telephone: 0608 810203. Key obtainable from chemist's shop opposite.

This small and intimate museum shows crafts, industries and schooldays in Charlbury.

CHIPPING NORTON
Chipping Norton Museum, New Street, Chipping Norton. Telephone: 0608 3342 and 41216.

This new museum in the former Baptist schoolroom has exhibitions of local interest including Roman remains (the 'Chipping Norton head') and objects associated with the town's tweed and brewing industries.

CLAYDON
Claydon Granary Museum, Butlin Farm, Claydon, Banbury OX17 1EP. Telephone: 029 589 258.

The displays, housed in a former granary, cowshed and cattle yard, show items used in homes, farms, offices and workshops in north Oxfordshire in the nineteenth and early twentieth centuries. There are tractors and other farm machinery and a 1912 steam roller.

FILKINS
Swinford Museum, Filkins, Lechlade. Telephone (chairman): 036786 365. Open by arrangement.

This fine collection of Oxfordshire agricultural, craft and domestic implements was established in the 1920s in a seventeenth-century cottage.

LONG HANBOROUGH
Oxford Bus Museum Trust, British Rail Station Goods Yard, Long Hanborough, Oxford. Telephone (secretary): 08677 4080.

This growing collection of buses dating from between 1915 and the 1960s has acquired most of its exhibits from the City of Oxford Motor Services but also includes buses from Hong Kong and Lisbon.

LONG WITTENHAM
Pendon Museum of Miniature Landscape and Transport, Long Wittenham, Abingdon OX14 4QD. Telephone: 086730 7365. Open only on weekend afternoons. Group visits by coach by written arrangement only.

In this museum fascinating model landscapes recreate the English countryside of the early 1930s. A village of thatched cottages and farm buildings is set amidst the hills and farmland of the Vale of White Horse. Accurately modelled trains pass over one of Brunel's timber viaducts in a Dartmoor setting.

OXFORD

Ashmolean Museum of Art and Archaeology, Beaumont Street, Oxford OX1 2PH. Telephone: 0865 278000.

The Ashmolean Museum was the first public museum in Great Britain. The nucleus of the museum was the collection of antiquities, natural history specimens, artefacts from foreign countries and other items accumulated by the two John Tradescants, father and son, which the younger Tradescant gave to Elias Ashmole in 1659. Ashmole offered the collection to Oxford University on condition that it provided a suitable building to house it. This was done and the original building in Broad Street (which now houses the Museum of the History of Science) opened in 1683.

The collections expanded over the years and benefactions enabled the Ashmolean to move to its present neo-classical building, designed by Charles Cockerell, in 1845. Much important archaeological material was acquired in the nineteenth century, notably from the excavations of Evans in Crete and Petrie in Egypt. The natural history and ethnographic collections were transferred respectively to the new University Museum and Pitt Rivers Museum. In 1894 a large extension to the building was constructed and collections of bronzes, ceramics and paintings were added to what had become a predominantly archaeological museum. In the twentieth century the Heberden Coin Room was opened, the Cast

Above: *The County Hall, Abingdon, houses the town's museum.*

Below: *Ashmolean Museum, Oxford.*

The dinosaurs in the University Museum, Oxford.

Collection was largely formed (now in a separate building) and the Oriental Collections were brought to Beaumont Street.

Today the Ashmolean's remarkably fine collections include, amongst many other things, British, European, Egyptian and Near Eastern archaeology; European paintings, drawings, prints and ceramics; sculpture and bronzes; coins and medals; Islamic art; Asian art and ceramics.

Bate Collection of Historical Instruments, Faculty of Music, University of Oxford, St Aldates, Oxford OX1 1DB. Telephone: 0865 276139.

This is England's most important collection of historical European musical instruments — brass, woodwind, percussion, keyboard — and also has a complete bow-maker's workshop and a full Javanese gamelan.

Museum of Modern Art, 30 Pembroke Street, Oxford OX1 1BP. Telephone: 0865 722733.

This gallery stages a changing programme of exhibitions, workshops, performances, films and lectures by artists, many of whom are from east European or Third World countries.

The Museum of Oxford, St Aldates, Oxford OX1 1DZ. Telephone: 0865 815559.

The Museum of Oxford consists of a series of displays, on two floors, showing life in Oxford from prehistoric times to the twentieth century. It shows plans and model reconstructions of medieval college buildings and some of the many religious foundations which disappeared after the Dissolution of the Monasteries in the reign of Henry VIII (chapter 4). Exhibits outline the story of both town and gown, through Saxon and medieval times, the Renaissance, the Civil War and the Restoration, to the scientific discoveries of the seventeenth and eighteenth centuries and the coming of industrialisation with William Morris (Lord Nuffield) and his motor cars.

Room settings have been arranged to show how Oxford people lived, from seventeenth-century students to the labourer's family in their tiny Jericho house and the don's grand drawing room in North Oxford.

Museum of the History of Science, Old Ashmolean Building, Broad Street, Oxford OX1 3AZ. Telephone: 0865 277280.

This museum is devoted to scientific instruments of every kind and is particularly rich in astrolabes, some of which date from the ninth century and are of Arab craftsmanship. Other treasures are microscopes, watches, surgeons' instruments and photographic equipment. The most popular exhibit is Einstein's blackboard, still covered in his calculations. The seventeenth-century building, the original home of the Ashmolean Museum, has lovely stained glass, warm oak staircases and fine paintings.

The Oxfordshire and Buckinghamshire Light Infantry Regimental Museum, Slade Park Barracks, Headington, Oxford OX3 7JJ. Telephone: 0865 716060.

The county regiment, now incorporated into the Royal Green Jackets, is well represented in this collection of medals, uniforms, badges and regimental silver.

Pitt Rivers Museum, South Parks Road, Oxford OX1 3PP. Telephone: 0865 270927.

Housed adjacent to the University Museum, through which it is reached, the Pitt Rivers Museum has one of Britain's leading collections of ethnographic and prehistoric specimens from all over the world, with particular emphasis on the cultures of Africa and the Pacific. Popular exhibits are the totems, shrunken heads and arms and armour. Other attractions are religious and cult objects, while at the Balfour Building in Banbury Road (telephone: 0865 274726) musical instruments may be seen and heard.

Rotunda Museum of Antique Dolls' Houses, Grove House, Iffley Turn, Oxford OX4 4DU. Open on Sunday afternoons in summer or by written appointment. Children under sixteen are not admitted.

This is a private collection of more than forty dolls' houses complete with furniture, crockery, silver, books, carpets and dolls, dating from between 1700 and 1900.

The University Museum, Parks Road, Oxford OX1 3PW. Telephone: 0865 272950.

This is the home of the university's scientific collections in entomology, geology, mineralogy and zoology and is very much a working museum. Many of the collections are second in importance only to those at the Natural History Museum in London. Skeletons of dinosaurs tower above other exhibits, which include examples of birds, mammals and reptiles from all over the world. There are also large fossil and gemstone collections. The display on the dodo gave Lewis Carroll the idea of using this bird in *Alice in Wonderland.* Columns made of different types of rock, busts of famous scientists and the huge glass and wrought iron roof give the building a strong feeling of Victorian Gothic.

UFFINGTON
Tom Brown's School Museum, Broad Street, Uffington SN7 7RA. Telephone: 036782 675.

This specialised museum illustrates the life and works of Thomas Hughes, author of *Tom Brown's Schooldays, Tom Brown at Oxford* and *The Scouring of the White Horse,* as well as showing background material from the White Horse area.

WALLINGFORD
Wallingford Museum, Flint House, High Street, Wallingford OX10 0DB. Telephone: 0491 35065.

The displays show a thousand years of the town's history from Saxon times to the present, with an exhibition on Wallingford Castle (chapter 4). Temporary exhibitions are also staged.

WANTAGE
Vale and Downland Museum Centre, The Old Surgery, Church Street, Wantage OX12 8BL. Telephone: 02357 66838.

A cloth merchant's house of the sixteenth and seventeenth centuries has been imaginatively converted and extended to house displays on life in Wantage and the Vale of White Horse from prehistoric times. There are also temporary exhibitions of work by local artists and craftsmen, a shop and a coffee bar. The displays illustrate the numerous archaeological sites of the Vale, such as the White Horse and Wayland's Smithy (chapter 3).

WITNEY
Cogges Manor Farm Museum, Church Lane, Cogges, Witney OX8 6LA. Telephone: 0993 72602.

Near Cogges church (chapter 5) and the river Windrush, Cogges manor house and its outbuildings make up a museum of farming, craft and industry, including unusual breeds of domestic animals. The complex includes the

Harvest supper at Cogges Manor Farm Museum.

Edwardian farmhouse, a dairy, garden and orchard, as well as the site of a deserted medieval village. Daily demonstrations are held of such rural activities as lacemaking, cookery, blacksmithing, candlemaking, hurdlemaking and shearing.

WOODSTOCK
Oxfordshire County Museum, Fletcher's House, Park Street, Woodstock OX7 1SN.

Telephone: 0993 811456.

This museum, the headquarters of Oxfordshire County Museums Service, is in a beautiful stone town house with a garden. As well as the permanent galleries which deal with the history, culture and archaeology of the whole county, there are temporary exhibitions on a variety of themes. There is a well stocked bookshop and Fletcher's House is sometimes also used for concerts.

The restored building at 26/7 Cornmarket Street, Oxford.

8
Other places to visit

Ardington Home Farm, School Road, Ardington, Wantage. Telephone: 0235 833302.

Part of the newly developed buildings on Ardington Estate, Home Farm houses many craft shops and industries including chair restorers, a sculptor and stone-mason, a clockmaker, an artist, picture framers and restorers, designers of wooden furniture and Ardington Pottery, which is in the nineteenth-century dairy.

Burford Garden Centre, Shilton Road, Burford. Telephone: 099383 3117.

At the Centre are a cactus nursery, a pottery and other craft workshops, and Cotswold knitwear can be purchased.

Combe Mill, Blenheim Sawmills, Combe, Oxford. Telephone: 08675 2652.

This Victorian sawmill on the Blenheim Estate has a working steam beam engine, the original Cornish boiler and a working forge.

Cooper's Shop and Marmalade Centre, 84 High Street, Oxford OX1 4BG. Telephone: 0865 245125.

Frank Cooper's 'Original Oxford Marmalade' is exported all over the world and the company has returned to its original home. As well as marmalade, the shop sells condiments, teas, speciality chocolates, mustard, china and sketches of Oxford.

26-7 Cornmarket Street and 26 Ship Street, Oxford.

Known for generations as 'Zac's', from Zacharias's outfitters which occupied the building from 1856 to 1983, the site has been renovated by its owners, Jesus College. A new frontage of English oak was inserted on the first floor and is clearly visible from the street. This has been left uncoloured to display the combination of ancient and modern craftsmanship. It contains a row of oak windows, replicas of the late fifteenth-century originals and like them unglazed, the glass being set further back into the room.

The Cornmarket Street building had to be completely dismantled and reconstructed, using as many of the ancient oak timbers as possible. No glue, nails or screws were used, only pegs, in all the structural timbers. Archaeologists have established that these buildings formed part of a late medieval inn with a central courtyard, an entrance in Ship Street and upper rooms overlooking both Cornmarket and Ship streets. There is now student accommodation on the third floor, and

Laura Ashley occupies the renovated shop. The rear part of the shop is what used to be the inn courtyard and, looking upwards and backwards from the ground floor, one can see fine fourteenth-century jettying, revealed by restoration. The upper sales floor was originally open to the roof, with no ceiling.

Cotswold Wildlife Park, Burford OX8 4JW. Telephone: 099382 3006. Off the A361 south of Burford.

Centred on a manor house, the wildlife park consists of 120 acres (49 ha) of gardens and parkland. Apart from its wonderful collection of animals, reptiles and insects, there are pony rides, a centre for rubbing animal brasses, train rides and an animal adoption scheme.

Cotswold Woollen Weavers, Filkins. Telephone: 036786 491. Between Burford and Lechlade, ¾ mile (1.5 km) off the A361.

This working weaving mill is housed in a splendid eighteenth-century barn. An historical and practical exhibition shows the history of weaving and wool, and there is a mill shop selling clothing, rugs, furnishings and gifts.

Didcot Power Station, Didcot OX11 7HA. Telephone: 0235 815111. Central Electricity Generating Board.

The power station offers a film and tour lasting about 1½ hours. Telephone for details. Applications to visit by groups or individuals must be made in writing.

Didcot Railway Centre, Didcot OX11 7NJ. Telephone: 0235 817200. Entrance through Didcot Parkway railway station.

The Great Western Society is recreating at Didcot the golden age of the Great Western Railway. In the original shed there are more than a score of steam locomotives, with a reconstructed station and broad-gauge demonstration. The society arranges a regular programme of 'steam days'.

Great Coxwell Tithe Barn, Great Coxwell. National Trust.

The barn was built in the early thirteenth century by Cistercian monks from Beaulieu Abbey in Hampshire, who had a cell here. It is made of Cotswold stone and roofed with stone tiles. It is 152 feet (46.4 metres) long, 44 feet (13.2 metres) wide and 48 feet (14.6 metres) high up to the ridge. Of particular interest is its timber construction, which is clearly visible from the inside. The barn was acquired by the National Trust in 1956.

Great Coxwell Tithe Barn.

Maharajah's Well, Stoke Row, Henley-on-Thames.

The well was a gift from the Maharajah of Benares and was most welcome in this small village above the water-line in the Chilterns. Work started in 1863 and it was opened a year later. It is 368 feet (113 metres) deep, just over the height of St Paul's Cathedral, and was dug entirely by hand. The superstructure is unaltered.

Oxford Brass Rubbing Centre, University Church of St Mary the Virgin, High Street, Oxford. Telephone: 0865 791829.

This centre contains a large collection of exact replicas of brasses from the Oxford area, from which visitors may take rubbings. It forms part of the historic Old Congregation House attached to the University Church. Ready-made rubbings and gifts are on sale.

Oxford Covered Market, between High Street and Market Street, Oxford.

This is one of Britain's oldest surviving covered markets, dating from 1773. Its shops include fruiterers, cafes, butchers, florists, delicatessens, tea and coffee shops, cheese shops, fishmongers, game dealers and woollen and fancy goods emporiums.

The Oxford Story, 6 Broad Street, Oxford OX1 3AJ. Telephone: 0865 728822.

Developed in conjunction with Oxford University, the Oxford Story introduces the visitor to university life and literally transports him or her, seated at a medieval student's desk, through the turbulent history of Oxford from medieval times to the present day by means of visual images and sounds. Visitors will learn how the many famous people connected with Oxford — monarchs, statesmen, martyrs, philosophers, scholars, writers, actors and artists — fit into the university story.

Rycote Chapel, near Thame. English Heritage. Off the B4013 about 10 miles (16 km) east of Oxford, 3 miles (5 km) west of Thame.

The chapel stands in Rycote Park, the site of a sixteenth-century mansion belonging to the Norreys family. Rycote was the scene of a battle during the Civil War and in the eighteenth century the house was burned down. The chapel of St Michael and All Angels was built as a chantry for Roger Quatremain, lord of the manor, and was completed in 1449. It is all of one architectural style and remains structurally unaltered. It is now in the care of English Heritage and, after restoration, looks much as it would have done to Quatremain. The majority of the pews are medieval, with two startling seventeenth-century additions. One has a canopy of almost Ottoman design, the other a minstrels' gallery. Another pew is equipped with a fireplace. The chapel's ceiling was painted with gold stars on a blue background in the seventeenth century. Its oldest possession is the font, probably twelfth-century, but remodelled.

Royal visitors to Rycote have included Elizabeth I in 1592, James I in 1616 and Charles I in 1625. Next to the chapel is a tree reputedly dating from Stephen's reign.

Waterperry Horticultural Centre, Waterperry, Wheatley, Oxford. Telephone: 08447 226 or 254. Signposted from Wheatley, 2 miles (3 km).

This horticultural college for women students was founded in 1932. It is set in 83 acres (34 ha) of parkland with gardens, herbaceous borders, lawns, riverside walks, alpines, glasshouses and trees. The house itself dates from the eighteenth century, and the nearby parish church is well worth visiting (chapter 5).

Wellplace Zoo, Ipsden, Oxford OX9 6AD. Telephone: 0491 680092 and 680473. Off the A4074 Oxford to Reading road, and the A423 Wallingford to Henley road.

This small zoo specialises in tropical birds and animals of kinds which are popular with children.

9
Oxford: the city and the university

THE CITY OF OXFORD

The name of the city is derived from 'ox' and 'ford': Oxford was the place where drovers brought their animals across the Thames. Oxford's coat of arms shows an ox walking over a river.

The Romans did not settle in the area that is now the city centre. It was not until Saxon times that Oxford became established and its present street plan shows its Saxon origins. The earliest written reference is in the Anglo-Saxon Chronicle of 912, and by 1066 it was estimated to be the sixth largest town in England. Several Saxon kings were born or died in Oxford and later the Plantagenets had a residence here, Beaumont Palace, where Richard the Lionheart was born in 1157. In the middle ages, however, the city declined as the new university flourished and from the mid thirteenth century the history of Oxford is largely that of the university.

Despite its antiquity and reputation for learning, modern Oxford does not live in the past. It is a thriving, noisy, cosmopolitan place, full of traffic, students, tourists and shoppers. It has a large polytechnic, a college of further education, several tutorial and secretarial colleges and many language schools. The population of Oxford is about 120,000, most of whom earn their living in education and tourism, printing and publishing, engineering, catering, brewing and the car industry.

To understand Oxford today it is essential to know something about the university, its history and its place in modern society.

OXFORD UNIVERSITY
History

Like Cambridge, Oxford University was never formally founded, hence the mixture of architectural styles, the spread of sites throughout the city and the lack of campus. It has existed in various stages of development since at least 1096, expanding rapidly after 1167 when all English students were expelled from Paris university. All early students lived in houses or hostels and were in holy orders.

Soon contention arose between them and the townspeople, who resented this invasion, and so began the 'town and gown' rivalries which lasted for centuries. This continual feuding led to several serious riots: after one in 1209 there was an exodus of students to Cambridge; another in 1355, known as the St Scholastica's Day Massacre, raged for two days and nights and left 63 students and thirty townsfolk dead.

Edward III intervened in favour of 'gown',

the university prospered and attracted endowments, and then specially built halls and colleges sprang up. In the thirteenth century Balliol, Merton and University colleges were founded, each claiming to be the university's oldest. Town life, though, steadily declined.

Under the Tudors Oxford became a centre of the English Renaissance with new colleges being founded on the sites of suppressed religious houses. There was a barbaric side, too, notably the destruction of priceless 'popish' manuscripts and the burning at the stake of the Protestant martyrs Latimer, Ridley and Cranmer in 1555-6.

Town and gown differences manifested themselves in the seventeenth century, when the city was largely Parliamentarian in sympathy and the university mainly Royalist.

The Martyrs' Memorial, Magdalen Street, Oxford.

During the Civil Wars Charles I lodged at Christ Church and Queen Henrietta Maria at Merton. After the Restoration Oxford became Charles II's temporary capital while the plague raged in London. During this reign leading Oxford scientists formed the nucleus of the future Royal Society.

In the eighteenth century, however, there was a period of corruption when teaching posts were little more than sinecures and students forsook learning for hunting and drinking. Then a written examination system was introduced in 1800 and under the Victorians there was a vast improvement in both academic and moral standards in Oxford.

In the 1830s the Oxford (or Tractarian) Movement came into being, led by Newman, Keble and Froude, in an attempt to bring the Church of England nearer to the teaching of the early Christian fathers.

Dons were allowed to marry in the mid nineteenth century and this brought an outbreak of building activity, particularly in North Oxford.

In 1871 the monopoly of the Anglican Church was broken with students of any or no religious persuasion being admitted.

The first women's college, Lady Margaret Hall, was opened in 1878 and others followed over the next decade, although women could not be admitted to degrees until 1920, even if they had been successful in the examinations.

The modern university

There are nearly ten thousand undergraduate and four thousand postgraduate students at Oxford at any one time, almost half of them being women. Any candidate with suitable qualifications may apply, regardless of class, age or nationality, entry being strictly by competition. Successful applicants come in roughly equal numbers from state and private schools and are considered for their social as well as their academic potential. Candidates must apply to and be accepted by a college, not by the university itself. Newcomers are not full members of the university until they have matriculated, usually during the first week of Michaelmas term, in the Sheldonian Theatre.

Lectures, classes and laboratory courses are provided by the university, tutorials by the colleges. The tutorial, Oxford's greatest strength, is a weekly meeting of one or more students with a tutor responsible for their progress. The three university terms, Michaelmas, Hilary and Trinity, last only eight weeks each and tuition is therefore very intensive.

The first degree is normally the Bachelor of Arts, even for scientists, for there is no Bachelor of Science degree, and the courses last three years, four for Classics. Degrees are awarded by the university, not by the individual colleges.

Examinations are taken in the Examination Schools in High Street, the majority in May and June, and full academic dress is worn. The first university examination is the First Public Exam, usually taken at the end of the first year, with the Second Public or Finals at the end of the course. Passes in the Bachelor of Arts degree are classified into firsts, upper and lower seconds, thirds and passes, a first or upper second being necessary to do research.

As at Cambridge and Dublin, no examination or research is necessary to obtain the degree of Master of Arts, which at Oxford is awarded seven years after matriculation provided that the graduate has paid his college dues during this period, and on payment of a fee. Master of Arts status confers membership of Convocation, a body which elects the Chancellor of the university and the Professor of Poetry.

Conventional higher degrees range from the one-year Master of Studies, through various other masters, to the Doctor of Philosophy. Higher doctorates exist but these are either restricted to members of the university of many years standing or awarded *honoris causa* at the annual Encaenia ceremony in June when about six prominent persons from all walks of life and from anywhere in the world are honoured by the university (see below).

Oxford holds degree days on nine Saturdays throughout the year, in the Sheldonian Theatre. There is no compulsion for graduates to have their degrees conferred at any specific time as they are not awarded by year, by college or by subject but as and when people care to receive them. The Vice-Chancellor presides, assisted by the two proctors, and candidates are brought forward to him by the college deans of degrees for admission, sometimes singly, sometimes in batches, depending on the degree. Some, notably MAs, are gently tapped on the head with a New Testament. This done, the participants leave the theatre,

change into gowns appropriate to their new status and re-enter the Sheldonian to great applause.

All Oxford ceremonies are still conducted in Latin, with an English translation being made available.

Creweian Benefaction

On the last Wednesday in June the Vice-Chancellor and prominent members of the university assemble to partake of the Creweian Benefaction before they attend the Encaenia ceremony.

Lord Crewe's benefaction consists of strawberries and champagne, served to senior university officials, doctors above the rank of DPhil and the distinguished people who are being awarded honorary doctorates at the Encaenia. The benefaction is paid for from the proceeds of £200 left in the will of Nathaniel, Lord Crewe (1633-1722), Bishop of Durham, and invested for that purpose. Once the strawberries and champagne have been consumed, the participants form themselves into a procession, adhering strictly to rules of precedence, and, led by the head of the city police, the university marshal, the verger and the bedels, set off for the Sheldonian Theatre.

The procession makes its way through the Bodleian Library's Catte Street gate, across Schools Quadrangle and into the Divinity School, where the honorands are left to await their summons while the rest continue into the theatre for the actual Encaenia ceremony.

A degree ceremony in the Sheldonian Theatre.

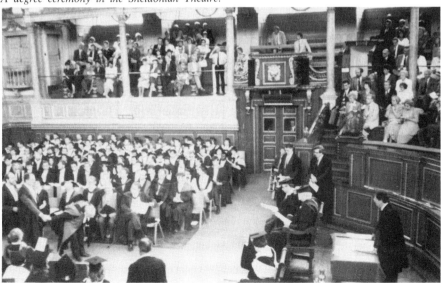

Encaenia

Inside the Sheldonian the Lord Mayor and Lady Mayoress, the Sheriff, the Lord Lieutenant of Oxfordshire and the audience consisting of other members of the university, employees and guests are listening to an organ recital. When the procession enters, the National Anthem is sung and the Chancellor opens the Congregation; this is normally the only time that he officiates at a ceremony.

After the honorary degrees are publicly approved, the bedels are sent off to escort the honorands from the Divinity School. Each is introduced in turn, with a Latin speech from the Public Orator, who explains why the candidate is to be honoured. The audience is provided with a bilingual programme so that all may follow what is going on.

After a speech of welcome and a handshake, the Chancellor gives the new doctor a scroll. Honorands over the centuries have included John Evelyn, Samuel Johnson, Mark Twain, Rudyard Kipling, Sir Winston and Lady Churchill, General Eisenhower, the Duke of Wellington, Helmut Schmidt, Mrs Indira Gandhi, Joseph Haydn, Andrès Segovia and Charlie Chaplin.

Then the winners of certain university prizes for Greek, Latin and English verse and prose and for historical essays recite extracts from their compositions and, lastly, either the Public Orator or the Professor of Poetry (they take it in turns) delivers the Creweian Oration, in English. This is a summary of all the appointments, retirements, obituaries, gifts and purchases, events and occasions of the past academic year.

The Oration over, the Encaenia is terminated by the Chancellor with the words *Dissolvimus hanc Congregationem*. He then leaves his throne and is conducted by the bedels from the theatre.

Encaenia is followed by a formal luncheon at All Souls' College, and then a garden party in the afternoon.

Sport at the university

Oxford and Cambridge sportsmen and sportswomen who represent their university against the other are awarded 'blues' (or 'half blues' for some sports) and are themselves known as Oxford or Cambridge blues. Such confrontations include the Varsity cricket match at Lord's cricket ground in London, the rugby match at Twickenham and various other contests throughout the year. The best known is the University Boat Race, which originated in 1829 and now takes place each spring on the Thames in London between Putney and Mortlake, a distance of 4¾ miles (6.8 km).

UNIVERSITY INSTITUTIONS

Although there is no campus or central building which is the actual university, there are several institutions which belong to the university rather than to any one college and most of them are well worth visiting. For the Ashmolean, Pitt Rivers and University museums, and the Museum of the History of Science, see chapter 7.

The Bodleian Library. Telephone: 0865 277000.

'The Bod' is one of Europe's oldest libraries, dating from 1602. In the fifteenth century, however, the university had already built a library over the Divinity School to house the magnificent collection of manuscripts donated by Humfrey of Gloucester,

The Encaenia procession entering Schools Quad.

Above: *Ceiling of the Divinity School, Oxford.*
Left: *Radcliffe Camera, Oxford.*

Henry V's brother, and today this part, Duke Humfrey's Library, is the oldest as well as the most beautiful of the Bodleian's reading rooms.

In the mid sixteenth century this early library was dispersed, largely because of political and religious upheavals, but in 1602 Sir Thomas Bodley refounded it. In 1610 Bodley arranged with the Stationers' Company that the library should receive a copy of each new publication and this still applies.

Extensions followed: Arts End in 1610-12, Selden End in the 1630s. In 1789 the Bodleian took over the first two floors of the Schools Quadrangle (1613-19) which originated as lecture rooms and examination schools; the subjects are still displayed over the doorways. In the 1860s James Gibbs's Radcliffe Camera (1749) was adopted as a reading room and in the twentieth century various smaller libraries came under the Bodleian's wing, together with the New Bodleian in Broad Street, which was completed in 1939 and opened by King George VI in 1946. Today the Bodleian owns around 4.5 million books and more than fifty thousand manuscripts, none of which may be loaned to anyone.

Admission to the book stack is strictly by

47

reader's ticket only, but conducted tours have been introduced which include visits to Duke Humfrey's Library, the Exhibition Room and the Divinity School. The charge includes an information pack on the Bodleian Library.

The Botanic Garden, High Street, Oxford. Telephone: 0865 276920.

Opposite Magdalen College at the far (east) end of High Street, the Botanic Garden was laid out on the site of an old Jewish cemetery, hence the name Deadman's Walk for the path which leads to it from Christ Church. It was founded in 1621 as a physic garden by Henry, Earl of Danby, who also endowed it. It is the oldest botanic garden in Britain and remains much as it would have looked to Pepys and Evelyn, who both mentioned it in their diaries.

In the south garden is a display of roses, tracing the origin of today's specimens from the wild variety. The present greenhouses date from 1970 and are open to the public in the afternoon.

The garden plays a vital role in the study of economic factors involved in plant growth in developing countries.

The Rose Garden, between the entrance and High Street, commemorates the discovery of penicillin in Oxford.

The Botanic Garden is an ideal spot from which to watch the efforts of punters on the Cherwell, which runs alongside.

The Divinity School

On display in one of Oxford's loveliest buildings are some of the Bodleian's most valuable possessions. Entry is in Schools Quadrangle, behind the bronze statue of the Earl of Pembroke; its vestibule, the Proscholium, is also known as the Pig Market from its use in Henry VIII's time.

Its treasures include the revised Magna Carta of 1217, the manuscript of T. E. Lawrence's *The Seven Pillars of Wisdom* and that of Kenneth Grahame's *The Wind in the Willows,* drafts of poems by Donne and Shelley, a note passed between Charles II and Clarendon and many other letters, poems and first folios.

The Divinity School was begun in 1427 and completed in 1483. Financed by public sub-scription, the crests and initials of contributors decorate its beautiful ceiling bosses. It has been variously used as the home of the Theology Faculty, as an armoury and in 1655 as a meeting place for the House of Commons. The Divinity School and its immediate neigh-bour, Convocation House, are still used for university functions.

Oxford University Press, Walton Street, Oxford. Telephone: 0865 512201.

The original press produced its first book in 1478 in premises in High Street; it is dated 1468 by mistake. In 1669 the Sheldonian Press started operating from the Sheldonian Theatre and in 1713 it moved to the newly built Clarendon Building, finally settling in its present home in 1830 when it changed its name to the Oxford University Press, or OUP. It continues to produce its academic titles under the imprint of the Clarendon Press. The OUP is owned by the Chancellor, Masters and Scholars of the university and is one of three presses permitted to print the Authorised Version of the Bible and the Book of Common Prayer, the Cambridge University Press and Her Majesty's Printers being the others. Major productions include the *New English Diction-ary* (the original edition running to 15,000 pages, all hand-set), the *Dictionary of National Biography* and the *New English Bible.* There are OUP showrooms in High Street and branches all over the world.

The Sheldonian Theatre, Broad Street, Oxford. Telephone: 0865 277299.

Not a theatre at all but the ceremonial hall of the university, the Sheldonian gets its title because its architect, Christopher Wren, used plans adapted from those of the ancient Roman theatre of Marcellus. It was named after Gilbert Sheldon, later Archbishop of Canterbury, who provided most of the money for its construction, and it was Wren's first major work, opened in 1669.

The principal matriculation ceremony and all the degree ceremonies take place here as well as meetings of Congregation, public lectures, occasional debates and many con-certs.

The Theatre's unusual architectural features include its wooden interior painted to resem-ble marble, the Proctors' boxes with lions holding Roman fasces in their mouths, and the painted ceiling. This depicts an allegory of Truth descending on the arts and sciences to help banish Ignorance from the university. Ignorance is represented by a black, snaky-haired hag above the organ case. The ceiling was painted in 1668 by Robert Streeter on 32 canvas panels and was brought to Oxford by barge along the Thames.

The painting and the attic floor above it are unsupported from below, being kept in place by enormous roof trusses. As it measures 70 by 80 feet (33.6 by 38.4 metres) and Wren had to rely on mathematical principles rather than steel girders, it is a wonderful achievement, visited by architects from all over the world.

The seventeen heads on the pillars round the Sheldonian and the Museum of the History of Science are known as the 'emperors' or the 'philosophers', but they represent no one in particular as they are merely boundary mar-kers in the classical style.

Left: *Sheldonian Theatre, Oxford.*
Below: *'Emperor's head' outside the Sheldonian Theatre.*
Bottom: *The ceiling painting and the organ in the Sheldonian Theatre.*

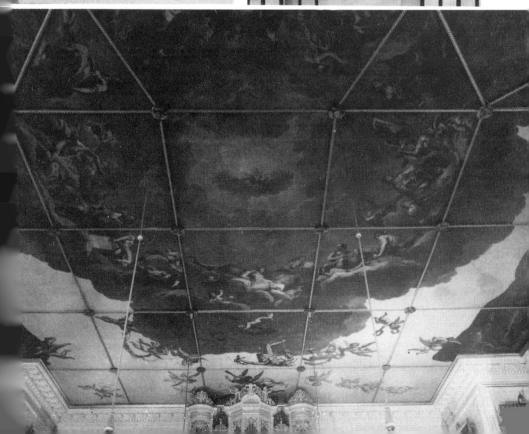

The University Chest

Today the University Chest is the name of the university's finance department, which issues computer-generated cheques decorated with tiny coffers. This is a reminder of medieval times when money and articles of value belonging to the university were stored in a secure chest, locked by a number of different locks, the keys of which were held by official 'clavigers'.

There have been a number of chests over the centuries. The first was set up in 1240 by order of the Bishop of Lincoln and was kept in St Frideswide's Priory. Another ancient one, which would once have been kept in the University Church, is now in the Ashmolean Museum. In it would have been stored the £3 0s 8d fine imposed on the city annually, and discontinued only in the 1980s. This fine was the reason that the University Chest was established in the first place. Not only was the chest a safe, but it also acted as a sort of bank for money-lending transactions and as a pawnshop.

In the office of the Secretary of the Chest today is a third chest, one of a pair bought in the late seventeenth century. It has five keys and is painted with the arms of all the colleges then in existence. In 1667 a system was instigated by which all deposits and withdrawals involving the chest were noted in two special ledgers and signed by the keyholders. One book stayed with the chest, while the other was kept by the Vice-Chancellor. The initial entries show that the university was worth £2360 13s 5d. In 1756 a bank account was opened and the entry *et sic remanent in cista nihil* entered in the ledgers to close them. Although 'nothing remained in the chest', its name lives on, both in function and in office.

WALKING TOURS OF THE CITY

These suggested routes are intended to give the visitor some idea of the extent and variation of the things to be found in central Oxford. It would not be practicable to visit all the buildings mentioned in one tour and so the tours are for orientation purposes only.

Tour one (from Carfax to Magdalen Bridge and back).

On the left side of High Street: the Covered Market; the Mitre Hotel; across Turl Street (diversion to Lincoln, Jesus and Exeter colleges); All Saints' church (now Lincoln College library); Brasenose College; St Mary the Virgin church (diversion to the Radcliffe Camera and the Bodleian Library); across Catte Street; All Souls' College; Queen's College; across Queen's Lane (diversion to St Edmund Hall); across Longwall Street; Magdalen College; Magdalen Bridge, with punts in season.

Cross over the High Street and walk back up it: Botanic Garden and the Rose Garden; across Rose Lane; block of shops and houses belonging to Stanford University; Eastgate Hotel; across Merton Street; Examination Schools; Frank Cooper's Marmalade Shop; University College, with Boyle plaque; across Magpie Lane; Oriel College; across Oriel Street; across King Edward Street, Shepherd and Woodward academic dress shop and outfitters; Carfax.

Tour two

From Carfax, follow the left side of St Aldates; Town Hall; Museum of Oxford (across to the right is the Information Centre); Christ Church (opposite is Pembroke College); turn left into the Memorial Gardens (opposite is Alice's Sheep Shop); into Christ Church Meadows; turn left, skirting Merton Field (diversion, if one turns right, into Deadman's Walk, along the old city wall, back into High Street near Botanic Garden); along lane passing Merton on one's right; into Merton Street and left to Corpus Christi College; right again to Merton; on leaving Merton, across and left into Magpie Lane; across High Street; through St Mary's church; round the Radcliffe Camera, and straight on; into Old Schools Quad; into the Divinity School, left into next quad; into the Sheldonian Theatre (climb the cupola for the best view of Oxford); left from the Sheldonian, into Broad Street; left into Museum of the History of Science; Exeter

Opposite: *Plan of Oxford city centre, showing the locations of the colleges and other places of interest. Key to colleges: 1 All Souls'; 2 Balliol; 3 Brasenose; 4 Christ Church; 5 Corpus Christi; 6 Exeter; 7 Green; 8 Hertford; 9 Jesus; 10 Keble; 11 Lady Margaret Hall; 12 Linacre; 13 Lincoln; 14 Magdalen; 15 Merton; 16 New College; 17 Nuffield; 18 Oriel; 19 Pembroke; 20 Queen's; 21 St Anne's; 22 St Antony's; 23 St Catherine's; 24 St Cross; 25 St Edmund Hall; 26 St Hilda's; 27 St Hugh's; 28 St John's; 29 St Peter's; 30 Somerville; 31 Trinity; 32 University; 33 Wadham; 34 Wolfson; 35 Worcester. Key to other places of interest; A Ashmolean Museum; B Bate Collection of Historical Instruments; C Bodleian Library; D Botanic Garden; E Carfax Tower; F Cathedral Church of Christ; G Church of St Mary Magdalen; H Church of St Mary the Virgin; J Church of St Peter in the East; K City Church of St Michael at the North Gate; L Cooper's Shop and Marmalade Centre; M 26-7 Cornmarket Street; N Divinity School; O Museum of Modern Art; P Museum of Oxford; Q Museum of the History of Science; R Oxford Brass Rubbing Centre; S Oxford Castle; T Oxford Covered Market; U The Oxford Story; V Oxford University Press; W Pitt Rivers Museum; X Sheldonian Theatre; Y University Museum.*

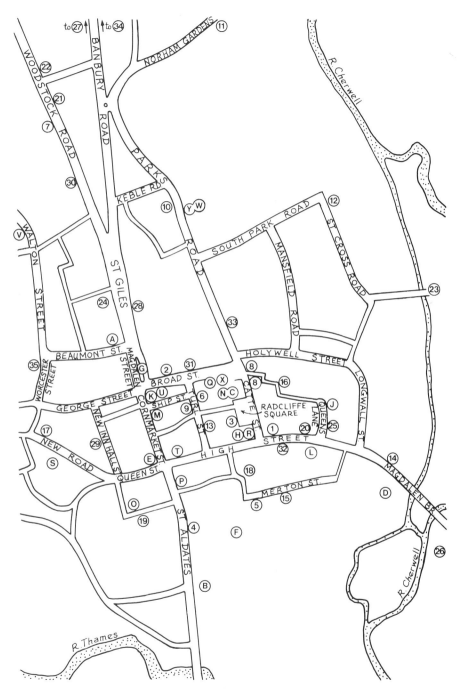

College; cross Broad Street to Blackwell's bookshop; Trinity College; Balliol College; St Mary Magdalen church; left into Cornmarket Street and back to Carfax.

Tour three

From Carfax, take right side of Cornmarket Street; Number 3, Painted Room; Laura Ashley Shop at corner of Ship Street; across Ship Street; St Michael at the North Gate church and Saxon tower; across Broad Street; St Mary Magdalen church; Martyrs' Memorial; cross to pavement on the right; look across St Giles' to the Randolph Hotel, Ashmolean Museum and Taylorian Institute; St John's College; turn into entry by the side of the Lamb and Flag, into Museum Road, at the end of which are University Museum and Pitt Rivers Museum; right to Keble College; cross to left-hand pavement; Parks Road, leading to Science Area; on the corner is Rhodes House; Wadham College; King's Arms public house; part of Hertford College; under Bridge of Sighs; into New College Lane; New College; back into New College Lane; left into Queen's Lane; follow Queen's Lane; St Peter in the East church (churchyard and crypt may be visited from St Edmund Hall); St Edmund Hall; High Street; across right into Logic Lane and into Merton Street (or, if lane closed, left into Merton Street itself); Merton College; right into Oriel Square; Oriel College; King Edward Street; left into High Street; Carfax.

Right: *High Street, Oxford.*
Below: *Rhodes House.*

10
The Oxford colleges

There are 35 colleges and five permanent private halls, the latter principally for members of religious denominations. Most colleges accept both undergraduate and postgraduate applications for most subjects, although seven are graduate colleges, of which one is for medical studies only. All colleges accept both men and women, apart from Somerville and St Hilda's, which are for women only.

The majority of colleges are open to the public from 2 pm until dusk although some are open all day, particularly during vacations. All university institutions are liable to close without notice so it is advisable to check in advance if it is important to visit one particular place. The oldest colleges are the most interesting as well as the most central and are dealt with at greater length here.

All Souls' College, High Street, Oxford OX1 4AL. Telephone: 0865 279379.

In 1438 Henry Chichele (pronounced Chitchlee), Archbishop of Canterbury, and Henry VI founded the 'College of All Souls of the Faithful Departed, of Oxford' in memory of all those who fell in the Hundred Years War. It consists of a Warden and Fellows, with no undergraduates, an arrangement unique until the appearance in the twentieth century of the graduate colleges. Members of All Souls', however, are not merely graduates, they are the cream of the academic world. Oliver Cromwell lodged at the college during his chancellorship in 1651-7.

The Front Quad is mid fifteenth-century, little altered, and the chapel (1447) on its north side has carved stalls, a hammerbeam roof with angels and a wonderful reredos. An archway leads to mid eighteenth-century Great Quad by Hawksmoor, a pupil of Wren, and on the north side is the Codrington Library (1756), one of Oxford's greatest. It has 150,000 volumes, including many manuscripts, some from the eleventh century, and Wren's designs for St Paul's Cathedral. The library itself is noted for its Wren sundial (1658) and its plasterwork and is a lovely venue for classical concerts. The hall, in the corner of Great Quad, is similar to the chapel and has a collection of portraits of All Souls' men, including the founder, all painted for posterity.

Once every century, on 14th January (the next time will be in 2001), the Ceremony of the Mallard takes place. The Fellows, led by a Lord Mallard in a sedan chair, holding a dead duck on a pole, go up on to the rooftops at night by torchlight looking for the ghost of a mallard which supposedly flew out of the foundations when the college was being built. As they go they sing their Mallard Song in remembrance of this bird.

Balliol College, Broad Street, Oxford OX1 3BJ. Telephone: 0865 277777.

Founded in 1263 by a Scottish nobleman, John de Balliol, as a penance for quarrelling with the Bishop of Durham, Balliol is one of Oxford's three oldest colleges. It is also one of the most important, in both numbers and influence, and has long been academically outstanding. It helped to spread the New Learning at the Renaissance. Very little of the early fabric remains as the college was altered and rebuilt in the eighteenth and nineteenth centuries, with the inclusion of a fine collection of gargoyles.

On entering Front Quad, the chapel (1857 by Butterfield) is on the north side, the library on the west. The chapel contains sixteenth-century glass and more by van Linge (1637), while the lectern and pulpit are also seventeenth-century, these early items coming from Balliol's demolished Tudor chapel.

The library is fifteenth-century, with a valuable collection of illuminated manuscripts and much heraldic glass. In the north-west corner of Front Quad is Salvin's Tower (1853) and the entrance to the hall (1877, Waterhouse), which contains an organ upon which weekly concerts are given.

Brasenose College, Radcliffe Square, Oxford OX1 4AJ. Telephone: 0865 277830.

Founded in 1509 by William Smyth, Bishop of Lincoln, and Sir Richard Sutton, on the site of Brasenose Hall, the college's curious name comes from its chief treasure, a door-knocker composed of a face with a large brass nose, and dating from the eleventh or twelfth century. This knocker was taken off to Lincolnshire from an earlier foundation in 1333 and did not return to Oxford until 1890. It was discovered in a girls' school which 'BNC' bought in order to repossess its nose. Fifty years later the school was resold at a substantial profit. The nose now hangs above High Table and there are smaller copies in the window glass, over the main doorway, round a High Street doorway and on the college seal.

Entrance is by the gate tower (1516), leading into Old Quad, with the early sixteenth-century hall with its panelling and plaster ceiling. In the middle of the east wall are the Stuart arms.

In Second Quad is the fifteenth-century kitchen from Brasenose Hall, and the chapel

Christ Church: the memorial gardens with Tom Tower beyond.

and library, both 1656-66. In the chapel is a window commemorating Louis XVIII's visit to Oxford in 1808, when he dined in hall. New Quad, on High Street, is late nineteenth-century by Jackson.

BNC has a good sporting reputation, particularly at rowing. The college boat is called the *Child of Hale* after a Lancashire giant who visited the college in the seventeenth century.

Christ Church, St Aldates, Oxford OX1 1DP. Telephone: 0865 276150. (Visitors' entrance through Memorial Gardens and Meadow Buildings.)

The word 'college' should never be included in Christ Church's title. It is sometimes called 'The House' from its Latin name, *Aedes Christi* ('House of Christ'). In 1525 Cardinal Wolsey founded Cardinal College, which did not progress far before Wolsey fell from favour. It was refounded by Henry VIII in 1532 and again in 1545, this time as Christ Church. Wolsey's kitchen is still in use.

Christ Church is unique in that its head is the Dean, both of the college and of the cathedral chapter; he is the only college head appointed by the Crown, and this is the only college with a cathedral as its chapel. Queen Elizabeth I visited and took great interest in her father's foundation, where Charles I and Charles II also resided, thus continuing its links with royalty.

The main entrance is by the Fair Gate in St Aldates, which has 48 coats of arms on its vaulted roof. Above it is Wren's Tom Tower

with a cupola housing Great Tom, a massive bell which booms out 101 times at 9.05 pm, a reminder of the original number of undergraduates and the time by which they had to be home. Inside, the enormous Tom Quad has a pool with a statue of Mercury in the middle; the Quad dates from the sixteenth and seventeenth centuries.

In the south-west corner is the hall staircase, a spectacular piece of Gothic revival from 1640, while the hall itself is Oxford's largest, measuring 115 by 40 feet (35.4 by 12.3 metres), and has carved and gilded hammer-beam roofing, arms and devices on its bosses, and one of the best portrait galleries, showing Christ Church members by Lely, Kneller, Reynolds, Gainsborough, Lawrence, Millais, Watts and Sutherland.

Through a passage in the north-east corner of Tom Quad is Peckwater Quad (1714) in Palladian style, with the college library (completed 1772), which is not normally open to the public except by prior arrangement. Its contents are priceless and include Wolsey's cardinal's hat and chair, John Evelyn's diary and much material relating to Lewis Carroll, who, as C. L. Dodgson, was a mathematics don here.

In tiny Canterbury Quad is the modern picture gallery, which is open to the public and contains paintings and drawings from the fourteenth to the seventeenth centuries. From Canterbury Quad an exit leads into Merton Street and Oriel Square.

Christ Church retains its strong ties with

Eton College and has produced no less than thirteen prime ministers. For the cathedral see chapter 5.

Corpus Christi College, Merton Street, Oxford OX1 4JF. Telephone: 0865 276700.

Corpus Christi was founded in 1517 by Richard Fox, Bishop of Winchester and confessor to Queen Catherine of Aragon. It is the smallest Oxford college and pleasantly eccentric. Corpus is the centre of Oxford tortoise life and holds a Tortoise Fair for charity each summer. Academically, the college has a sound reputation for classics.

Corpus is known for its sundial (1581) in Front Quad. It is topped by a perpetual calendar from 1606. The early sixteenth-century library contains classical manuscripts from the tenth century and early printed books. In the chapel is an altarpiece of the Adoration of the Shepherds, believed to be by Rubens, and the founder's enamelled crozier. Past the chapel entrance is Fellows' Quad, Oxford's smallest quadrangle and little more than a cloister; it was added in 1706-12.

Corpus Christi is unique in that it still has its old plate, whereas that of other colleges was handed over to Charles I at the onset of the Civil War.

On the opposite side of Merton Street is Beam Hall, one of the old medieval student halls which was acquired by Corpus in 1553.

Exeter College, Turl Street, Oxford OX1 3DP. Telephone: 0865 279600.

Founded in 1314 as Stapeldon Hall by a Bishop of Exeter, Robert de Stapeldon, Exeter College received its present name in 1586. It is known as the 'Westcountryman's college' because of its founder's origins and because it awards a number of scholarships to students from the west of England.

Despite its medieval foundation, Exeter College today is principally Victorian. The only surviving medieval building is the original gatehouse (1432) called Palmer's Tower, said to be haunted by a headless man who throws himself from it.

The college hall (1618) is noted for its roof which is made of Spanish chestnut. The mid nineteenth-century chapel was modelled on the Sainte Chapelle in Paris and has a tapestry of the Adoration of the Magi and stained glass windows all designed and executed by the Pre-Raphaelites.

Green College, Woodstock Road, Oxford OX2 6HG. Telephone: 0865 274770.

A new foundation originally planned as Radcliffe College, Green is next door to the eighteenth-century Radcliffe Infirmary, Oxford's first teaching hospital. It takes its name from Dr and Mrs Cecil Green, who financed the new college. Dr Green, a Mancunian, established Texas Instruments in Dallas.

Green College is a postgraduate medical college, the only one to specialise exclusively in a single subject. It incorporates the Radcliffe Observatory, paid for by the royal physician John Radcliffe and designed by Wyatt in the 1770s, with a polygonal tower topped by a globe which Atlas and Hercules support; it is reminiscent of the Temple of the Winds at Athens.

Hertford College, Catte Street, Oxford OX1 3BW. Telephone: 0865 279400.

Hertford's history goes back to the 1280s when it was called Hart Hall; its name changed to Hertford College in 1740. It fell into decay in the nineteenth century and finally collapsed in a pile of rubble, to be refounded in 1874.

Hertford is not outstanding architecturally apart from Jackson's famous 'Bridge of Sighs', which was constructed in 1913 to connect two parts of the college. The oldest buildings are the former chapel of Our Lady at Smithgate (1521), now the Junior Common Room, with a sculpture of the Annunciation over its doorway, and the few surviving buildings from old Hart Hall (mid sixteenth-century) which are used for lectures.

Evelyn Waugh's novel *Brideshead Revisited* depicts Hertford as it was in the 1920s when he was an undergraduate there.

Corpus Christi: the sundial and perpetual calendar.

The Bridge of Sighs at Hertford College.

Jesus College, Turl Street, Oxford OX1 3DW. Telephone: 0865 279700.

Known as the Welshman's college from its founder in 1571, Dr Hugh Price, Jesus continues to attract students from Wales and is the seat of the Professor of Celtic Studies. Until the middle of the nineteenth century, when nonconformists were finally allowed into the university, Jesus was severely restricted in its choice of members, few Welshmen being Anglican.

The oldest buildings are the sixteenth-century Turl Street frontage and the entrance into Front Quad, which has the hall on the west and the chapel on its north side. The chapel (1621) is Jacobean Gothic, restored in the nineteenth century, and has a bronze bust to a former student, T. E. Lawrence (of Arabia). The arms on the screen (1693) are those of a former principal and benefactor, Sir Leoline Jenkins. On 1st March, St David's Day, a service is held here in Welsh.

Among the portraits in the hall (also Jacobean) are those of Elizabeth I, under whose patronage Dr Price founded Jesus, Charles I by Van Dyck, Charles II supposedly by Lely, as well as two modern English graduates of the college, T. E. Lawrence and Lord Wilson (Harold Wilson). To the south is a carved oak screen (1634) decorated with monsters which look like Welsh dragons.

Inner Quad (1639-1713) was paid for by Welsh donations and has attractive little gables. To its north is Third Quad, rebuilt and enlarged in 1947.

Keble College, Parks Road, Oxford OX1 3PG. Telephone: 0865 272727.

Keble was built in the 1870s as a memorial to John Keble, founder-member of the Oxford Movement. Its purpose was to provide 'economical' education for men who would otherwise have been unable to afford it. It was a Christian foundation with ideals based on those of the Church of England but there were no restrictions upon denomination. It was built by public subscription.

The original buildings of 1868-82 are by William Butterfield, to a rather startling design in red brick, with decorative patterns of other colours. Keble was the first college to have corridors in place of staircases.

The very large multicoloured chapel has mosaics and carvings, with yet more brickwork, tiles and stained glass. Its main feature, in a special little side chapel built to house it, is Holman Hunt's painting 'Light of the World'. Other copies of it are in Manchester and St Paul's Cathedral in London.

Keble is a building which one either loves or hates; John Ruskin felt obliged to alter the course of his morning walk to avoid it, but today it is admired by enthusiasts for Victoriana.

Lady Margaret Hall, Norham Gardens, Oxford OX2 6QA. Telephone: 0865 274300.

Lady Margaret Beaufort, the mother of Henry VII, was a scholarly lady and so her name was chosen by the first principal of Oxford's first college for women. 'LMH' was founded in 1878 with the help and support of the Warden of Keble, Dr Talbot. That year the Association for the Higher Education of Women was founded by a few dons in order to supervise the work of women students. As the Association became increasingly successful it became independent and self-governing.

The college was officially opened in 1879 in a family house in Norham Gardens, with nine students. The original buildings were first added to in the 1880s by Basil Champneys, with subsequent twentieth-century enlargements, which include Sir Giles Gilbert Scott's chapel (1932) in Byzantine style; it houses a fifteenth-century Flagellation attributed to Gaddi and a Burne-Jones triptych.

Linacre College, South Parks Road, Oxford OX1 3JA. Telephone: 0865 271650.

In 1962 Linacre College was established by the university as a graduate society for research into any subject. It was named after Sir Thomas Linacre, founder of the Royal College of Physicians in 1518. Linacre became a self-governing college in 1965. It was originally located in St Aldates, between Christ Church Memorial Gardens and the police station, in buildings which had once been used by St Catherine's Society before that college was founded in 1963. At that period every college member lived out as there was no accommodation provided. In 1977 Linacre transferred to Cherwell Edge, the former St Frideswide's Convent at the end of South Parks Road, and backing on to the University Park.

Lincoln College, Turl Street, Oxford OX1 3DR. Telephone: 0865 279800.

The college was founded in 1427 by Richard Fleming, Bishop of Lincoln, and remains pleasantly medieval in appearance because it was poorly endowed and could not afford to 'improve' its ancient buildings. The tower and gateway with rooms above it date from the founder's time. The original chapel bell hangs in Front Quad and is rung before evensong. The hall (1437) has a timbered roof with Oxford's only remaining octagonal louvre, constructed so as to allow smoke to escape. Two important buildings belong to Lincoln College: one is the Mitre, once a famous old coaching inn and now a restaurant. The college has now repossessed most of the former hotel rooms for student accommodation. The other is All Saints' church (1710), the former city church which was declared redundant and converted for its new role as Lincoln College library in 1975.

Magdalen College, High Street, Oxford OX1 4AU. Telephone: 0865 276000.

Pronounced 'Maudlin', the college was founded in 1458 by William of Waynflete, Bishop of Winchester, on the site of the thirteenth-century hospital of St John the Baptist.

Magdalen's bell-tower (1492-1509) is a symbol of Oxford worldwide. Every May Morning (1st May) at six o'clock crowds gather on Magdalen Bridge to hear the college choir sing its hymn to spring. Afterwards the city bells ring out and there is morris dancing through the streets and squares.

Magdalen's entrance lodge leads into St John's Quad with its open-air pulpit. Each year, on the Sunday nearest St John the Baptist's day (24th June) a sermon based on the life and works of the saint is preached from this pulpit. It is specially draped with an embroidered velvet cloth and chairs are set out on the grass below, including the Vice-Chancellor's throne. Formerly the ground was strewn with grass, rushes and branches in memory of the Baptist's preaching in the wilderness. The sermon is open to members of the public and lasts about half an hour.

To the left are the Grammar Hall (1614), St Swithun's Buildings (1880-4), the New Library Building (1849) and Longwall Quad (1928-30). Ahead is the late nineteenth-century President's Lodging and, across to the right, Founder's Tower, the college's original entrance. Through Muniments Tower is the fifteenth-century Cloister Quad with 'hieroglyph' mons-

The colonnaded New Building at Magdalen College.

ters on its buttresses. On the south side are the hall and chapel. The hall, reached by a flight of steps, has an oak roof, fine linenfold panelling and portraits of Magdalen men.

Access to the chapel is normally restricted to the ante-chapel with its original stalls, fifteenth-century misericords, an interesting painted fifteenth-century chest, several ancient brasses and the tomb of Waynflete's father, Richard Patten, brought here when Wainflete church in Lincolnshire was destroyed in the nineteenth century.

Through the cloisters is the colonnaded New Building (1733), its severity softened by wistaria, and to its left is the Deer Park, or Magdalen Grove, the home of the college deer since about 1700. To the east lie Addison's Walk and Magdalen Meadows (see chapter 2).

Across the High Street, between the Rose Garden and the Botanic Garden, is the Daubeny Building (1854), used for graduate accommodation.

Merton College, Merton Street, Oxford OX1 4JD. Telephone: 0865 276310.

Walter de Merton, Chancellor of England, founded the college in 1264. Its statutes were copied by subsequent foundations, notably Cambridge's first college, Peterhouse, in 1284. Merton was the earliest purpose-built college, as opposed to the already existing assortment of houses and hostels.

The tower of Merton College chapel.

Entrance is by the Gatehouse Tower (1418), which is like a tiny castle with statues of the founder and Henry III and carvings of John the Baptist and various animals.

The Fitzjames Gateway is known for its zodiac carvings; above its doorway are the Queen's Rooms, used by Henrietta Maria during the Civil War and in the next reign by Catherine of Braganza.

Mob Quad has the wonderful Old Library (1337-8), the oldest in regular use anywhere. Its treasures are manuscripts and books (including a chained example), fifteenth-century astrological instruments, with an astrolabe said to have been used by Chaucer, a thirteenth-century oak chest and beautiful sixteenth-century glass. As there is plenty of stained glass but no electricity it is possible to get a good idea of what life was like in the medieval university. The Old Library is said to be haunted by both Duns Scotus and Sir Thomas Bodley. For a nominal charge visitors are shown round the Old Library by the verger, who explains everything in fascinating detail; no visitor to Oxford should ignore this opportunity.

Those interested in medieval glass should see Merton chapel, whose historic windows bear the arms of several monarchs and members of the English aristocracy. In the ante-chapel are monuments to famous Oxonians and a massive green marble font given to the college by a Tsar of Russia.

New College, New College Lane, Oxford OX1 3BN (also another entrance in Holywell Street). Telephone: 0865 248451.

Despite its name, New College was founded in 1379 by William of Wykeham, with the title of 'St Mary College in Oxford'. As there was already a St Mary's College (later Oriel) the nickname 'New' college remained. The college's title should always be 'New College', never just 'New'.

The founder's original designs were so well executed that they have been little altered since and the college inspired the layout of several later foundations.

The gatehouse (1386) is reached by New College Lane, Max Beerbohm's 'grim ravine'. In the same year Front Quad was completed, the first in all Oxford. The Cloister and Bell Tower (1400) are famous for their gargoyles, often reproduced as souvenirs for tourists.

The ante-chapel has some of the city's best memorial brasses, 23 in all, mostly from the middle ages. The arresting sculpture of 'Lazarus Rising from the Dead', by Epstein, is said to have given Nikita Khrushchev a sleepless night after a visit to New College. The window (1778-85) of the Adoration of the Shepherds by Sir Joshua Reynolds shows the artist himself as one of the company.

Oriel College: Front Quad and porch.

The chapel itself (1386) is remarkable for its amusing series of fourteenth-century misericords, while to the left of the altar, in a glass case, is the gold and enamelled crozier which belonged to William of Wykeham. There is also an El Greco painting of St James.

New College hall, one of the best in Oxford, is reached by stairs from Front Quad and is the oldest in the university (1386); it has linenfold panelling (1533) and nineteenth-century stained glass with heraldic motifs. The Long Room, once the college's communal lavatory, is now used for recitals and exhibitions.

New College garden was built, like the rest of the college, on a disused corner belonging to the city, possibly the site of a plague pit. It contains a surviving stretch of the old city wall and it was part of the founder's contract with the city fathers that the college should keep up this section of the wall. So well was this done that it is one of the few remaining portions. Every three years the Lord Mayor inspects the wall, standing on the top, dressed in all his finery. The mound in the middle of the garden has nothing to do with burials but was added to make a focal point.

Nuffield College, New Road, Oxford OX1 1NF. Telephone: 0865 278500.

Endowed by and named after the motor-car magnate Lord Nuffield, the former William Morris, the college aims to 'encourage postgraduate research especially, but not exclusively, in the field of social studies', with the idea of forging links between industry and academe. Nuffield, however, was heard to refer to his college as 'that bloody Kremlin'.

The college was constructed on the site of canal wharves, where earlier had been Robert D'Oilley's castle bailey. Of traditional honey-coloured stone, in a 'Cotswold-Byzantine' style, Nuffield has a tower and spire covered in copper. The tower contains the library instead of bells, and there is no formal chapel; instead a room has been set aside for worship.

Oriel College, Oriel Street, Oxford OX1 4EW. Telephone: 0865 276555.

Founded in 1326 by Edward II, Oriel was Oxford's first royal foundation, although, strictly, it was only refounded by the king: his almoner, Adam de Brome, was the first founder in 1324. Adam was also rector of St Mary the Virgin church, where he is buried.

The college was built on the site of several smaller halls and is entered from Oriel Street. Through the doorway one is immediately confronted by the imposing porch topped by two canopies and statues of Edward II and Charles I. Above the kings, under another canopy, are the Virgin and Child; all is seventeenth-century craftsmanship.

The porch leads to the hall (1642) with a fine hammerbeam roof; the chapel is from the same year. Back Quad contains the lovely library by Wyatt.

In Oriel's senior common room the Oxford Movement was born in the 1830s and the college is also the home of the Rhodes scholarships, which are awarded each year to sixty or more exceptionally gifted applicants from the English-speaking world under the terms of the will of Cecil Rhodes, an Oriel man who made a fortune in the South African diamond industry and gave the name of Rhodesia to what is now Zimbabwe.

Rhodes died in 1902 and, apart from the scholarships, left a huge amount of money to Oriel, £10,000 of which was to go to 'increase the dignity and comforts of the high table'. The Rhodes Building's High Street frontage was designed by Champneys in his own particular version of seventeenth-century styles.

Pembroke College, Pembroke Square, Oxford OX1 1DW. Telephone: 0865 276444.

The college was founded in 1624 and named after the university's Chancellor at the time, the Earl of Pembroke. It claims King James I as its founder. Although it is the successor of the medieval Broadgates Hall which was on the same site, its only surviving building from those times is the senior common room, to the right of Front Quad.

Pembroke's chapel is early seventeenth-century, renovated in 1973, with late Victorian glass most noticeable in the Charles I and Founder's windows. The hall is also Victorian and its portraits include one of Queen Anne by Kneller.

Although it is one of the smaller and less well endowed colleges, Pembroke has been very fortunate in attracting the goodwill of the wealthy McGowin family of Alabama who financed, among other things, the new library.

Pembroke's most famous student was Samuel Johnson, the dictionary pioneer, who was so poverty-stricken while at Oxford that he could scarcely afford shoes and sometimes had to stay in his rooms for lack of them. He stayed at Pembroke only about a year, but it holds his memory dear and preserves the massive teapot he used. The university later awarded him an honorary degree in place of the one he was too poor to obtain in his undergraduate days.

The Queen's College, High Street, Oxford OX1 4AW. Telephone: 0865 279120.

Named after Philippa of Hainault, wife of Edward III, the college was founded by her chaplain, Robert de Eglesfield. Although it dates from 1340, the college has no medieval or Tudor buildings, the earliest being seventeenth-century and in the classical style. The library (1696) is one of the most important as well as loveliest in Oxford, with more than 100,000 volumes including four Shakespeare folios and a first edition of Milton's *Paradise Lost*. The chapel (1719) is a popular venue for lunchtime and evening concerts open to the public.

The Queen's has connections with the north of England, particularly Cumbria. Because most students were unable to get home for Christmas and New Year festivities, the college developed some interesting customs which still survive. Two of the best known are the Boar's Head and the Needle and Thread ceremonies and, according to the founder's instructions, members of Queen's are summoned to dinner by trumpet.

The college is one of Oxford's best known landmarks for one of the city's main bus stops is outside. In the cupola over the gateway stands a statue (1734) of George II's queen, Caroline of Ansbach.

St Anne's College, Woodstock Road, Oxford OX2 6HS. Telephone: 0865 274800.

The college opened in 1879 with 25 female home students, becoming a society for 44 members in 1893. In 1942 it became St Anne's Society, and in 1952 a college. The buildings are all twentieth-century, the earliest being Hartland House, finished in 1938 to a design by Sir Giles Gilbert Scott. Before this students met in hired rooms. The original building was extended in 1951 to provide teaching and common rooms and accommodation. The hall, with three hundred places, followed in 1959. The 1964 Wolfson Building won a prize from the Royal Institute of British Architects and the Founder's Gatehouse (1966) a commendation from the Civic Trust.

St Antony's College, Woodstock Road, Oxford OX2 6JF. Telephone: 0865 59651.

This postgraduate college was founded in 1948 by a wealthy French businessman, Antonin Besse, because of the high regard in which he held the Oxford graduates in his employment. At the founder's request a number of places are reserved for French nationals.

The site was once an Anglican convent, suitably adapted, to which have been added the 200-seat hall and the common rooms (1970). A Centre for Japanese Studies (1980), endowed by the Nissan Corporation, is attached to the college.

St Catherine's College, Manor Road, Oxford OX1 3UJ. Telephone: 0865 271700.

Situated away from the city centre, near the Cherwell, 'Catz' is one of Oxford's largest colleges. Its origins go back to a student society for 'men of limited means' in 1868, which became St Catherine's Society in 1930; the present college was built in 1960. Everything, including the cutlery, was designed by the Danish architect Arne Jacobsen.

College members are equally divided into scientists and arts students, and St Catherine's is unusual in that it does not possess its own chapel, nearby St Cross church being used instead. It does, however, have an 80 foot (25 metre) bell-tower.

The hall, with its slate floor and oak furnishings, and its three tapestries, is the largest in the university, seating 365 diners. An original feature is the Music House in the south-west corner of the site.

St Cross College, St Giles, Oxford OX1 3LZ, and St Cross Road. Telephone: 0865 278490.

Established by the university as a society for postgraduate studies in 1965, the college started in a Victorian school in St Cross Road. In 1979, to mark their centenary, Blackwell's, the Oxford booksellers and publishers, contributed a large amount of money to St Cross, and with this and further endowments it was able to lease Pusey House in St Giles (with the exception of the chapel) and by 1981 had converted it into a college. Theological studies continue at Pusey House under the wing of St Cross, and the original St Cross site is also still in use.

St Edmund Hall, Queen's Lane, Oxford OX1 4AR. Telephone: 0865 279000.

Affectionately known as 'Teddy Hall', the college was named for St Edmund of Abingdon, who lectured in Oxford in the late twelfth century. It dates from 1238 and is the only independent survivor of the numerous halls and hostels which sprang up in the middle ages; it took full college status in 1957. The college is entered through a small gateway in Queen's Lane leading into Front Quad, which has as its focal point an ancient well. Front Quad was built over several different periods from the sixteenth to the twentieth century and it is a successful combination of all of them.

As at Lincoln College, a former parish church has been adapted to form the college library. This church, St Peter in the East, dates from the twelfth century and has a Norman crypt which may be visited (see chapter 5). The library is open to readers 24 hours a day.

In the High Street St Edmund Hall has some modern extensions, which, far from being out of place, blend in well with the existing range of buildings dating from the fourteenth century onwards.

St Hilda's College, Cowley Place, Oxford OX4 1DY. Telephone: 0865 276884.

Founded in 1893 by Miss Dorothea Beale, principal of Cheltenham Ladies' College, St Hilda's started in Cowley House, Cowley Place, as a community of women students. In 1894 it became St Hilda's Hall and in 1926 received its collegiate status.

In 1898 a south wing was added to Cowley House, with another in 1909. In 1921 Cherwell Hall was purchased and renamed St Hilda's South. The brick-built Burroughs Building appeared in 1934, with a library and student rooms above it, while the Wolfson Block (1964) has further accommodation. The Sacher Block and Garden Building were both built in 1971. St Hilda's most attractive feature is its pleasant grounds running down to the Cherwell.

St Hugh's College, St Margaret's Road, Oxford OX2 6LE. Telephone: 0865 274900.

Founded in 1886 as a hall by Miss Elizabeth Wordsworth, Principal of Lady Margaret Hall and niece of the poet, St Hugh's was first located at 24 Norham Road and its members were four impoverished women students. It became a college in 1911 and moved to its present site in 1916. The buildings were used as a military hospital in 1939 and the students transferred to Holywell Manor until 1945.

The earliest buildings, from 1916, are in eighteenth-century style, with the Mary Gray Allen Wing added in 1928. The Moberly Library was completed in 1936, the old library becoming Mordan Hall. A special room in the main building serves as the college chapel. Modern additions are the red-brick New Building (1966) and the 1967 Wolfson Building.

Exeter College chapel seen from Trinity College.

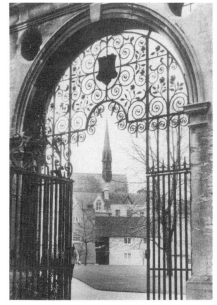

The Shelley Memorial in University College.

St John's College, St Giles, Oxford OX1 3JP. Telephone: 0865 277300.

This, one of the richest and most academically successful of Oxford colleges, was founded in 1555 by Sir Thomas White, a wealthy London merchant. It incorporates the Cistercian St Bernard's College, founded in 1437 and suppressed by Henry VIII. In 1579 the piece of land in front of St John's was purchased and walled in; it remains as Oxford's only surviving parvis.

The gatehouse gives access to Front Quad with the hall (1500) and chapel (1530) on its north side. The hall was enlarged in 1616 with subsequent alterations and restoration, but it retains its original collar-beam roof. The chapel was remodelled by Blore in 1843 and has late Victorian stained glass and reredos. In it are buried two former college presidents, Archbishops Laud and Juxon.

Through a central arch is Canterbury Quad with the library (1596-8), the remainder having been constructed between 1631 and 1636. The cloisters on either side were suggested and paid for by Laud and are adorned by statues of Charles I and Henrietta Maria, both by Le Sueur. The library, which was extended in 1977, has some ninety thousand volumes, including the only complete copy of Caxton's illustrated edition of Chaucer's *Canterbury Tales,* and also several letters written by Jane Austen.

Beyond Canterbury Quad is St John's garden, originally laid out by 'Capability' Brown, and now among the largest and most pleasant in Oxford.

Modern extensions to the college are the North and South (Dolphin) Quads and the startling but attractive Sir Thomas White Building (1976) housing the junior and middle common rooms, the college bar and student accommodation.

St Peter's College, New Inn Hall Street, Oxford OX1 2DL. Telephone: 0865 278900.

St Peter's was founded in 1929 by Francis Chavasse, Bishop of Liverpool and previously rector of the church of St Peter le Bailey which is now the college chapel; the rectory is now the college library. In the chapel are a few relics from the old church: a sixteenth-century chest, a seventeenth-century chair and some monuments. There is also a memorial window to Bishop Chavasse, showing him with his pet tortoise.

The entrance (1797) was built for the Oxford Canal Company and the early nineteenth-century Master's Lodgings in Bulwarks Lane were the company's headquarters. The rest of the college buildings are twentieth-century.

Somerville College, Woodstock Road, Oxford OX2 6HD. Telephone: 0865 270600.

Founded in 1879 and named in honour of

the Scottish mathematician Mary Somerville, Somerville Hall became a college in 1894. Squeezed in between Little Clarendon Street and the Radcliffe Infirmary, it is hardly visible from the street. The range of buildings covers the period 1879 to 1967. Somerville's claims to fame are its single-sex status and its two graduates who became prime ministers, Mrs Indira Gandhi (of India) and Mrs Margaret Thatcher.

Trinity College, Broad Street, Oxford OX1 3BH. Telephone: 0865 279900.

Trinity was founded in 1555 by Sir Thomas Pope on the site of the thirteenth-century Benedictine Durham College, which had been suppressed in 1544. The remains of Durham College may still be seen in Durham Quad, where the chapel, library and hall are situated.

The chapel is unusual in that it was built by a college president, Dr Bathurst, in 1691. It has much fine woodcarving, said to be by Grinling Gibbons, and a ceiling painting of the Ascension by Pierre-Berchet. Trinity's Garden Quad has a range of Wren buildings on its north side; he designed them in 1665 while working on the Sheldonian Theatre across Broad Street, and they were completed in 1682.

In Broad Street is Kettell Hall, built in the seventeenth century as a private residence for the eccentric president Kettell as far away from his college as was practical.

University College, High Street, Oxford OX1 4BH. Telephone: 0865 276602.

Known as 'Univ', the college was first endowed in 1249 by William of Durham, who left £206 14s 4d to maintain at least ten Masters of Arts. Univ is one of Oxford's three oldest colleges but its claim that its founder was Alfred the Great is without historical truth. Nevertheless the college held millennial celebrations in 1879 and still uses what is thought to be Alfred's coat of arms.

When entering the college look up at the lovely fan vaulting and coats of arms in the entrance, then turn right to see the Shelley Memorial, sculpted by Onslow Ford in 1894. The statue was destined for the British Cemetery in Rome but was rejected by the authorities there and so now stands in Shelley's old college rather than at his burial place. Even though the poet was one of Univ's most famous students he did not complete his course, being sent down in 1811 for writing a pamphlet entitled *The Necessity of Atheism*.

Radcliffe Quad (1716-19) was named after another former student, Dr John Radcliffe, Court Physician, after whom the Radcliffe Infirmary, John Radcliffe Hospital, Radcliffe Camera and Radcliffe Square are named. His statue stands above the gatehouse.

From Radcliffe Quad a small gate leads into Logic Lane, which forms part of Goodhart Quad (1962), with bold timber framing. To the north-east of this is Cecily's Quad (1974). These two quads were named after a former master of the college and his wife.

Wadham College, South Parks Road, Oxford OX1 3PN. Telephone: 0865 277900.

In the early seventeenth century a Somerset couple, Nicholas and Dorothy Wadham, decided to found a college. Nicholas, however, died in 1609, and so Dorothy was left to become the actual founder in 1612. She bought the site of an Augustinian friary and building started on Wadham in 1613. It was so well planned that very few alterations have been necessary to the college since the Wadhams' day, apart from extension and modernisation.

The ante-chapel has a seventeenth-century wooden clockface reputedly donated by Wren, who was an undergraduate and then Professor of Astronomy here. Among the flagstones are numbered slabs, said to mark where skeletons of Augustinian friars were re-interred during the construction of the present chapel. Wadham hall has interesting woodcarving and is haunted by a very persistent tall grey monk.

Wolfson College, Linton Road, Oxford OX2 6UD. Telephone: 0865 274100.

Established in 1966, Wolfson incorporated the embryo Iffley College and was named after Sir Isaac Wolfson, the great benefactor of both Oxford and Cambridge universities through donations from the Wolfson Foundation. The college also received substantial assistance from the Ford Foundation and specialises in postgraduate studies in the natural sciences. Wolfson was built on 10 acres (4 ha) of land by the Cherwell. Opened in 1974, it is the largest graduate college in Britain, with over three hundred students.

Worcester College, Worcester Street, Oxford OX1 2HB. Telephone: 0865 278300.

Although Worcester College itself dates only from 1714 when it was founded by Sir Thomas Cookes, its oldest buildings come from a thirteenth-century foundation, the Benedictine Gloucester College. These early fifteenth-century buildings are on the south side of Main Quad and were houses built by the various Benedictine communities which sent students to Oxford. The coats of arms of the individual abbeys are over each doorway.

Entrance is by a Hawksmoor gateway (1736) into Main Quad, with a central lawn and cloister along the east side. To the north are the chapel (rebuilt 1791) designed by Hawksmoor, and the hall (1784), whose ornate plaster ceiling (1783) is by Wyatt. Pump Quad, entered from the south-east corner of Main Quad, is mainly fifteenth-century.

Worcester College library is rich in works of early drama, seventeenth-century manuscripts and books which once formed part of Charles I's library, together with many manuscripts inherited from Gloucester College.

The college grounds are pleasant and surround a lake stocked with waterfowl and a large garden complete with woodland. At the east end of the garden, bordering on Hythe Bridge Street and Gloucester Green, are twentieth-century accommodation blocks.

Permanent private halls

These are Campion Hall, Brewer Street (for members of the Society of Jesus); Greyfriars, Iffley Road (giving priority to members of the Franciscan order); St Benet's Hall, St Giles (mainly for Benedictines); Mansfield College, Mansfield Road; and Regent's Park College, Pusey Street, a Baptist foundation. The first three accept men only.

Famous Oxonians and their colleges

Where more than one college is given, the first is the undergraduate college, the second the college where the person had a fellowship.

Addison, Joseph: Queen's.
Alexander of Tunis, Earl: Trinity.
Amis, Kingsley: St John's.
Arnold, Thomas: Corpus Christi.
Attlee, Clement: University.
Auden, W. H.: Christ Church.
Bannister, Sir Roger: Exeter (later Master of Pembroke).
Beecham, Sir Thomas: Wadham.
Beerbohm, Sir Max: Merton.
Belloc, Hilaire: Balliol.
Bentham, Jeremy: Queen's.
Betjeman, Sir John: Magdalen.
Blake, Admiral: Wadham.
Bodley, Sir Thomas: Merton and Magdalen.
Boult, Sir Adrian: Christ Church.
Bridges, Robert: Corpus Christi.
Buchan, John: Brasenose.
Burton, Richard: Exeter.
Campion, St Edmund: St John's.
Canning, George: Christ Church.
Carroll, Lewis: Christ Church.
Cary, Joyce: Trinity.
Churchill, Lord Randolph: Merton.
Clarke, Sir Kenneth: Trinity.
Day, Sir Robin: St Edmund Hall.
Day-Lewis, C.: Wadham.
Donne, John: Hart Hall (Hertford).
Edward, the Black Prince: Queen's.
Edward VII: Christ Church.
Edward VIII: Magdalen.
Eliot, T S.: Merton.
Evelyn, John: Balliol.
Flecker, James Elroy: Trinity.
Florey, Lord: Magdalen and Queen's.
Fox, Charles James: Hertford.
Fraser, Lady Antonia: Lady Margaret Hall.

Fullbright, Senator James: Pembroke.
Galsworthy, John: New College.
Gandhi, Mrs Indira: Somerville.
Gibbon, Edward: Magdalen.
Gladstone, W. E.: Christ Church.
Graves, Robert: St John's.
Green, Graham: Balliol.
Grey, Earl: Balliol.
Guthrie, Sir Tyrone: St John's.
Haig, Field Marshal Earl: Brasenose.
Halley, Edmond: Queen's.
Hampden, John: Magdalen.
Heath, Edward: Balliol.
Hemery, David: St Catherine's.
Henry V: Queen's.
Hobbes, Thomas: Hertford.
Hopkins, Gerard Manley: Balliol.
Hughes, Thomas: Oriel.
Huxley, Aldous and Julian: Balliol.
Johnson, Dr Samuel: Pembroke.
Lancaster, Sir Osbert: Lincoln.
Landor, W. S.: Trinity.
Laud, Archbishop: St John's.
Lawrence, T. E.: Jesus and All Souls'.
Lewis, C. S.: University.
Locke, John: Christ Church.
Lovelace, Richard: Worcester.
MacKenzie, Sir Compton: Magdalen.
Macmillan, Harold: Balliol.
MacNeice, Louis: Merton.
Morris, William: Exeter.
Nash, Beau: Jesus.
Newman, Cardinal: Oriel.
North, Lord: Trinity.
Olav, King of Norway: Balliol.
Penn, William: Christ Church.
Peel, Sir Robert: Christ Church.
Pitt, William (the Elder): Trinity.
Raleigh, Sir Walter: Oriel.
Rattigan, Terence: Trinity.
Rhodes, Cecil: Oriel.
Rusk, Dean: St John's.
Ruskin, John: Christ Church.
Salisbury, Lord: Christ Church.
Sayers, Dorothy L.: Somerville.
Shaftesbury, Lord: Christ Church.
Shelley, Percy Bysshe: University.
Sidney, Sir Philip: Christ Church.
Smith, Adam: Balliol.
Southey, Robert: Balliol.
Swift, Jonathan: Hertford.
Swinburne, Algernon: Balliol.
Taylor, A. J. P.: Oriel.
Thatcher, Margaret: Somerville.
Tolkien, J. R. R.: Exeter and Merton.
Tyndale, William: Hertford.
Vaughan, Henry: Jesus.
Waugh, Evelyn: Hertford.
Wesley, John: Lincoln and Christ Church.
Wilson, Lord (Harold): Jesus and University.
Wren, Sir Christopher: Wadham and All Souls'.
Wycliffe, John: Balliol.

11
Events and customs

Lying near the centre of England, Oxfordshire has absorbed customs and practices from all of its ancestral roots, Celtic, Anglo-Saxon, medieval and modern. It has, however, little that is not found in other counties, apart from the university ceremonies and events, most of which have their origins in the middle ages and have survived since then as living entities, rather than as revivals. Many Oxfordshire happenings are seasonal rather than tied to any one date, and so it is advisable to enquire at the Tourist Information Centre, St Aldates, Oxford OX1 1DY (telephone: 0865 726871) or the Thames and Chilterns Tourist Board, Market Place, Abingdon (telephone: 0235 22711) for confirmation.

Some events take place every so many years, examples being the Mallard Ceremony at All Souls' College (see chapter 10), which happens every century, and the inspection of the remains of the city wall in New College, by the Lord Mayor and Vice-Chancellor, which takes place every third year. At Abingdon on days of national rejoicing buns are thrown from the County Hall.

Conversely, some events which appeal to the general public are so frequent that it would be impracticable to list them, notably concerts and recitals all the year round, fêtes and street fairs with morris dancing during the summer months, and funfairs in September and October. Events are listed here chronologically in an Oxfordshire calendar. Morris dancing is dealt with separately at the end of the chapter.

New Year
On New Year's Day each year the Needle and Thread Gaudy takes place at the Queen's College. It consists of the Bursar going round the tables and giving each fellow and guest a needle threaded with silk, saying 'Take this and be thrifty'. The needle and thread are a pun on the name of the college founder, Robert de Eglesfield, as translated into French: *aiguille* and *fil*.

January
On 14th January, once every century, the Mallard Ceremony takes place at All Souls' College (chapter 10).

February
Towards the end of the month Torpids, or bump races, take place on the Isis (Thames). Torpids are only a preliminary to the more important Eights Week and are sometimes referred to as 'Toggers' in old books on the university.

Lent
East Hendred and Brightwell-cum-Sotwell have traditional Shrovetide songs (chapter 12).

Easter
Radley, near Abingdon, revived the custom of Clipping the Church in 1965. 'Clipping' is an old word for embracing, and the congregation holds hands to form a ring around the outside of the building.

April
On 23rd April the city dignitaries proceed to the Painted Room in Cornmarket Street, Oxford, where they drink the health of Shakespeare, whose birthday it was. It is also St George's Day.

May Day
It has long been the custom to celebrate May Day as the arrival of spring. An emphasis on blossom and sunshine has been grafted on to an older Celtic celebration of coming fertility. In many parts of Britain the election of a May queen and king and the carrying of garlands have all but died out. In Oxfordshire there have been some attempts at revival and there are two notable survivals.

At Charlton-on-Otmoor the village children make little wooden crosses which they cover with flowers and take to church. Inside the church is a large cross, made of clipped yew, which hangs on the rood-screen until the following May Day. A garland of flowers is made by the children and put up on the screen.

At six o'clock on May Morning the choir of Magdalen College, Oxford, sings a hymn to spring, *Te Deum Patrem Collimus*, on the top of the college's 144 foot (44 metre) tower. The hymn was not adopted until the late eighteenth century, although it is thought to have been written by a fellow of Magdalen about 1660. It is performed on only three sides of the tower, as a choirboy is said to have plunged to his death from the fourth.

In pre-Reformation times a requiem mass was said from the top of the tower for the soul of Henry VII, and today's ceremony may be an echo of this custom. After the hymn singing, Magdalen's bells ring out and are joined by all the other bells throughout the city. There is morris dancing around the town centre, and punting expeditions on the Cherwell. Oxford's pubs and restaurants open early for breakfast. By eight o'clock signs of fatigue begin to appear as many of the revellers have been up all night.

May

In late May five days are devoted to Eights Week, a social as well as a sporting occasion. This is the highlight of the Oxford rowing year when crews from each college row against each other in a series of bump races, a system which evolved at Oxford and Cambridge because the rivers Isis and Cam are too narrow for boats to race side by side. The object is to catch up with the boat ahead to give it a gentle bump. This achieved, both crews drop out of the race, while the winner moves up a section to race other successful eights in the same manner. The winning eight at the end of the week is known as the Head of the River and is much acclaimed.

Ascension Day

After a service, the vicar, choir and parishioners of the church of St Michael at the North Gate go round the parish armed with willow wands with which they beat the boundary stones. Their progress may be charted by the chalk alterations which they make to the date of previous beatings, and their route takes them round some of the most famous university buildings such as the Bodleian Library and the Clarendon Building.

Whitsun

At Bampton the Great Shirt Race, in which teams dressed in flowing garments push makeshift vehicles like prams on a tour of the

The choristers of St Michael's church beating the bounds.

local hostelries, is accompanied by the first-rate Bampton morris men. A collection is taken and the money given to charity.

At Shenington, near Banbury, the church is strewn with grass on Whitsunday and on the Sunday following.

Corpus Christi

On the feast of Corpus Christi, elsewhere largely a Roman Catholic feast, the clergy and choir of Magdalen College process round the cloisters before going into the chapel for a service. As they are attired in all their ecclesiastical finery and the host is carried before them in a pyx under a canopy, it is a most impressive sight, reminiscent of pre-Reformation England.

June

On the nearest Saturday to 19th June the residents of Abingdon's Ock Street elect their mayor (chapter 12). On the Sunday after 24th June the Wall Sermon is preached from the open-air pulpit at Magdalen College (chapter 10). On the Wednesday of the last week of June the university holds its Crewian Benefaction and Encaenia ceremony (chapter 9). On the first Monday after 29th June, Yarnton holds its Auction of Mowing Rights (chapter 2) while at the end of the month there is a festival of music and the arts at Dorchester Abbey.

July

During the first two weeks Music at Oxford stages a Handel in Oxford Festival at various venues round the city. Around this time the Sheriff's Races are held on Wolvercote Common, together with a dog show, Sealed Knot combats and similar entertainment.

September

In Oxford St Giles' Fair, one of England's greatest, takes up all of the city between Magdalen Street and the beginning of the Banbury and Woodstock Roads, and the buses are re-routed. The fair is held on the first Monday and Tuesday after the first Sunday (unless the first is itself a Sunday). On the third Thursday of September is Thame Agricultural Show, a one-day event with a fair which lasts for three days. Other September fairs are held at Chipping Norton, Bampton, Witney, Henley-on-Thames, Abingdon, Banbury and Wallingford.

October

On the first Saturday morning of Michaelmas Term (somewhere in the middle of the month) the university matriculates its new members in the Sheldonian Theatre.

In the last week of October Oxford Round Table stages a giant firework display for charity in South Park at the bottom of Headington Hill.

December

On Christmas Eve Bampton has a mummers' play and on Boxing Day a similar event takes place at the public houses in Headington Quarry.

On Boxing Day, from the fourteenth century until the 1960s, the Boar's Head Dinner took place at the Queen's College. The festivities, which include the singing of the Boar's Head Carol, now take place the week before Christmas, and old college members are invited.

Morris dancing

The name morris derives from 'Moorish', implying 'foreign'. It is possible that this form of dance came to England with the Normans, although it was known in Europe before 1066. A morris side normally consists of eight dancers but the number may vary. They are usually men and wear white knee breeches and fancy shirts, straw or top hats decorated with flowers or ribbons, garters, bells round the knees, and sometimes a waistcoat or tabard. They carry staves which they clash together, and dancing is accompanied by an accordion or, less frequently, by fiddle, flute or tabor. There is written evidence that morris in Oxfordshire dates back to the Restoration, and almost certainly well before: indeed Bampton claims to have danced since the fourteenth century and this is likely to be a conservative estimate.

It was formerly an exclusively working-class activity, a means of both earning a little extra money and seeing something of the neighbourhood, but today it is performed by both manual workers and professional men. Unusually, Spelsbury once had a women's side but it was disbanded about 1830.

By the close of the nineteenth century morris was all but extinct. Then Cecil Sharp saw a side of unemployed labourers dancing on Boxing Day 1899. This stimulated Sharp's interest in folk dance and music in general and led to a revival throughout the English-speaking world. Sharp and his followers travelled the British Isles in search of folk music and dances and made them into a noble and respectable part of the national heritage. Once revived, morris dancing spread, along with its rival and relation the Sword Dance.

Oxfordshire remains one of the leading morris counties, strongholds being at Headington, Abingdon, Bampton and Wheatley.

The main occasions when morris dancers are likely to be seen performing are on May Morning at Oxford (see above), at Abingdon on the feast of St Edmund (the nearest Saturday to 19th June) and at Bampton on

Magdalen College tower, where the hymn to spring is sung on May Morning.

Spring Bank Holiday and at Whitsun (chapter 12). Elsewhere morris men often dance at street fairs, carnivals, ox roasts, fêtes and similar occasions.

One impressive event is the Election of the Mayor of Ock Street, in Abingdon. This is done by means of a ballot, the votes being cast into a wooden box. The new mayor, who holds office for only the one day, is 'danced in' all over the town, and then there is a celebration supper. This custom was revived in 1938 after a lapse of half a century. It is believed to have started in 1700 after a fight between Ock Street residents and the other Abingdonians.

12
Towns and villages

ABINGDON
Early closing Thursday; market day Monday.

Abingdon, though now in Oxfordshire, was once the county town of Berkshire. Situated on an impressive sweep of the Thames, it is popular with boating enthusiasts and day trippers from Oxford. Near Abingdon Bridge is the Old Gaol (1805), now an arts centre. Bridge Street leads to Market Square and the imposing late seventeenth-century County (or Town) Hall, the upper storey of which houses Abingdon Museum (chapter 7). It was designed by a Burford man, Christopher Kempster, and shows a strong Wren influence.

In East St Helen Street is the parish church (chapter 5) and, within its precincts, three sets of almshouses. Long Alley, facing the west front, is the largest and oldest, founded in 1446 by the Guild of the Holy Cross. It has tall chimneys and a wooden gallery running its entire length. Brick Alley is to the south and was rebuilt in 1718, while Twitty's Almshouses were built by Charles Twitty for six poor people.

Historically, the most important buildings in the town are those of Abingdon Abbey. This complex may be visited (chapter 4). New Abbey buildings include a fine hall used for social events.

Two important streets are Stert and Ock Streets, both named after local rivers. In June the Mayor of Ock Street is elected for the day, with celebrations and morris dancing (chapter 11). To the north spreads Victorian Abingdon, centred on Albert Park. Abingdon School is the descendant of seventeenth-century Roysse's Grammar School, which began in the present Guild Hall.

ADDERBURY
Adderbury, south of Banbury, has warmly tinted ironstone cottages and stately houses. Adderbury is divided into two parts, East and West, by the Sor Brook, the focal points being the lovely church (chapter 5) and the green, both in East Adderbury. On the green are the seventeenth-century Rookery, where Lord Montague, William of Orange's minister, once lived, and Adderbury House, the home of John Wilmot, Earl of Rochester, the infamous Restoration poet. The manor house has diamond-shaped brick chimney stacks, and opposite are the seventeenth-century Grange and a largely medieval tithe barn. Beyond the brook lie the lanes and cottages of West Adderbury.

ARDINGTON
East of Wantage lies Ardington with its twin model village, Lockinge, both planned, restored and rebuilt by Lord Wantage for the Lockinge Estate workers. Lord Wantage also restored existing cottages instead of tearing them down, so the overall impression is of

Long Alley Almshouses, Abingdon.

Victorian Tudor. Ardington's church, although twelfth-century, was somewhat over-restored in 1847. It has a medieval squint in the chancel and memorials to the Clarke family, who held Ardington manor for over five centuries before moving from Ardington House (chapter 6) to Betterton House nearby. The statue of a kneeling woman is by Baillie, who designed Nelson's Column.

ASCOTT-UNDER-WYCHWOOD

The three villages which have 'under Wychwood' appended to their names, Ascott, Milton and Shipton, are so called after the royal forest of Wychwood, which once stretched some 12 miles (19 km) from Bladon to Burford. The name means 'Hwicca's wood' in Saxon, and parts remain today, despite dis-afforestation in 1857. The Whit Hunt, also of Saxon origin, was an annual event; its successor, the Whit Fair, was suppressed by the Duke of Marlborough in the mid nineteenth century because it had become unruly.

Ascott-under-Wychwood lies in the Evenlode valley, a little grey stone village with a Norman church. A section of a neolithic stone barrow excavated here has been reconstructed in the County Museum at Woodstock. About fifty bodies were found, the majority having died in their twenties, some showing evidence of a disability similar to spina bifida.

BAMPTON

Early closing Wednesday.

Formerly known as Bampton in the Bush, this small town was once important enough to be the centre of Bampton Hundred and was famous for its horse fair. The church of St Mary the Virgin, of Norman or possibly Saxon origin, has good examples of craftsmanship from all the great architectural periods. There is a battered effigy of a fifteenth-century knight, probably a Talbot. The parish was unusual in that until the nineteenth century it had three vicars, each with a separate house and churchwarden. Each held office for four months, and the results are evident in the parish register entries and in the local expression 'to quarrel like the vicars of Bampton'.

Bampton Castle, of which only a few fragments built into Ham Court survive, was built by Aymer de Valence, Earl of Pembroke, in the fourteenth century.

Bampton remains a centre of tradition and folklore and has produced many morris dancers. On Whit Monday the Great Shirt Race is held, commemorating the events of AD 784, when Ethelred the Shirtless pursued the Bamptonians in order to clothe himself. The race is of nineteenth-century origin, revived in 1952, and so called because entrants must wear long garments. The race raises a considerable amount for charity.

BANBURY

Early closing Tuesday; market days Thursday and Saturday.

Banbury, Oxfordshire's second largest town, is of Saxon origin although most of its buildings date from the seventeenth century onwards. Its livestock market is the largest in Europe, and Banbury cheeses were mentioned by Shakespeare. The town's speciality is the Banbury cake, similar to the Eccles cake.

The first reference to Banbury Cross appeared in the eighteenth century, although the nursery rhyme that mentions it must be much earlier. The 'fair lady' is variously identified as Celia Fiennes, the seventeenth-century traveller, or Queen Elizabeth I. The present cross (1859) is spire-shaped and decorated with statues (1914) of Queen Victoria, Edward VII and George V.

Banbury Castle was destroyed in the seventeenth century, and the fine medieval church was blown up to avoid repairs in 1792. A shopping centre occupies the castle site, and a new St Mary's church was built in the 1790s.

In High Street is the nineteenth-century White Lion, with a shopping precinct in its courtyard, and in Bridge Street is a supermarket flanked by the startlingly white columns of its predecessor, a Baptist chapel. In Parsons Street is the sixteenth-century Reindeer Inn, its enormous sign jutting out over the street. Banbury Museum (chapter 7) is near the cross.

BICESTER

Early closing Thursday; market day Friday.

Pronounced 'Bister', the name shows the Roman origin of this market town. It prospered in the sixteenth and seventeenth centuries, a period of great building activity. Some timber-framed work survives, mainly around Market End, the survivors of several eighteenth-century fires; other old houses remain in Sheep Street. A decline followed, mainly due to agricultural depressions, although Bicester has remained a centre for hunting and horse-riding people and the associated trades. The Royal Air Force station opened in 1917, and there is a large Army ordnance depot and much new housing development.

The Market Place is of interest and the medieval St Eadburgh's church has some Pre-Raphaelite glass. Bicester Priory stood nearby in Old Palace Yard, but its only remains are fourteenth-century carvings in the church.

BURFORD

Early closing Wednesday; market day Saturday.

Known as the 'Gateway to the Cotswolds', Burford consists largely of a long main street rising up from the Windrush, little spoiled by the crowds who come here. It is still a centre for local crafts like leatherwork and making woollen goods.

Near the bridge are a row of almshouses (1457, rebuilt 1828) and Burford Grammar School, endowed by Symeon Wysdom in 1576. On the right, going up the hill, is Burford Priory, once the home of Speaker Lenthall. Rebuilt in the early nineteenth century, it is now a convent. Burford is justifiably proud of its great 'wool' church (chapter 5). Notice also the town's fairy-tale roof line. See chapter 7 for the Tolsey Museum.

CHARLBURY
Early closing Thursday.

The centre of this small town in the Evenlode valley is largely stone-built, with historic inns such as the Bull and the Bell (about 1700). The thirteenth-century church tower can be seen from afar and in the well kept churchyard are many fine table tombs and a sundial of 1776. The church, St Mary's, dates from Norman times but in the nineteenth century it was drastically restored and the interior was whitewashed. Furnishings include a pillar alms box and a parish chest 8 feet (2.4 metres) long. There is an impressive Jacobean oak staircase. Around St Mary's are stone-roofed houses, many covered in wistaria or other creepers.

In Market Street is the Corner House, now the local museum (chapter 7) and in Playing Close is a Jacobean-style fountain (1897) commemorating a visit by Queen Victoria.

CHARNEY BASSET
Early closing Thursday.

Charney is a very rural community of thatched and slated cottages, the only amenities being the post office stores and the public house. St Peter's church is Norman, or possibly Saxon, with a Norman doorway and a tympanum showing a man holding two dragons, both biting his arms. The manor of Charney belonged to Abingdon Abbey and the abbot lived in the manor house. This very attractive building has stone-arched windows and oak-beamed ceilings and now belongs to the Quakers.

Nearby is Cherbury Camp, a prehistoric earthwork constructed like a hillfort on flat marshland (chapter 3). A legend says that King Canute once lived here, but this is without basis.

CHIPPING NORTON
Early closing Thursday; market day Wednesday.

Chipping Norton is the highest place in the county. Its history goes back before Domesday, but most of the surviving buildings are eighteenth-century or later. The September Mop Fair was formerly a hiring fair where employees carried tokens of their occupations.

The town has not been commercialised, its main features being stone-built pubs and hotels such as the Bunch of Grapes, the White Hart, the Blue Boar and the Crown and Cushion.

In Spring Street is the theatre, while further along is Church Street with good seventeenth-century almshouses and St Mary's church. The chancel and aisles of St Mary's show thirteenth-century work, but it is the fifteenth-century nave which impresses, for it is one of the best in the county. The great Decorated window in the south aisle probably came from Bruern Abbey at the Dissolution, and there is other medieval, Tudor and Stuart glass. In 1549 the vicar protested against Edward VI's first Prayer Book and was hanged from his church tower as a troublemaker.

CLIFTON HAMPDEN
Early closing Tuesday.

Named after the family of which John Hampden was a member, this old-fashioned village has thatched and timbered cottages. Its small church of St Michael and All Angels stands overlooking the Thames, which draws many visitors here. Across from the village is the Barley Mow inn, made famous by Jerome K. Jerome in *Three Men in a Boat* (1889). Although badly damaged by fire in 1975, the thatched pub has now been restored to its former loveliness. At Clifton Hampden lived Sarah Fletcher who lies in Dorchester Abbey. She hanged herself here in 1799 on learning that her husband intended marrying an heiress and her ghost has been sighted at regular intervals since then.

COTTISFORD

Immortalised as Fordlow in Flora Thompson's *Lark Rise to Candleford,* Cottisford has no memorial to its best loved inhabitant. Flora, who was born here in 1877, did not start her trilogy on Oxfordshire life in the 1880s and 1890s until she was sixty. Apart from some modern council houses, Cottisford is much as she would have known it. Her own home remains, as does the school, now a private house.

St Mary's church has neither tower nor spire, but there is a priest's stone seat with a piscina to one side and a stone coffin in the chancel wall. A brass shows a fifteenth-century knight and lady, with eight sons and five daughters.

COWLEY

Cowley, 'Cufa's clearing', is now very much an Oxford suburb, best known for its Austin Rover car factory and its shopping centre. Nevertheless, around St James's church is the Beauchamp Lane conservation area. The late twelfth-century church has a chancel arch and

Thatched cottages at Dorchester-on-Thames.

font from that time, and in the fifteenth century its squat tower with gargoyles was added. By the nineteenth century Cowley's population had increased so much that St James's narrowly escaped demolition as being too small. In 1864 Street added a new north aisle and raised the existing roof.

St Luke's church was the gift of an old boy of the parish school, William Morris, later Lord Nuffield. Morris started making bicycles in Longwall Street, Oxford. In 1912 he made his first car, and in 1921 his first inexpensive mass-produced model was produced in the former military college at Cowley. So successful did Morris Motors prove that Morris became a millionaire and Oxford's greatest modern benefactor, making gifts and endowments such as medical professorships and readerships and Nuffield College itself. This Cowley boy has had the most profound effect on modern Oxford.

DIDCOT

Didcot's railway junction was the reason why it developed into a town and was written about by John Betjeman. It has become partly a dormitory town for workers at the Atomic Energy Research Establishment at Harwell, Culham Laboratory and Oxford, but there is an older Didcot clustered round the old rectory, thatched barns and timbered schoolhouse. St Peter's church is medieval and contains the canopied tomb of an unknown ecclesiastic, possibly Ralph de Dudcote, Abbot of Abingdon. For the Didcot Railway Centre see chapter 8.

DORCHESTER-ON-THAMES

In glorious countryside where the Sinodun Hills meet the Thames, this site has been settled since at least Roman times, and the surrounding district since about 2500 BC. There was a small Romano-British town here (chapter 3) and the Saxons made Dorchester the centre of their see of Wessex, when Birinus founded a cathedral here in AD 635. The cathedral was superseded by what is now Dorchester Abbey (chapter 5), which is the highlight of a visit, although the entire village is noteworthy, particularly the High Street. Some buildings are medieval and timber-framed; others are of brick or stone. Dorchester's inns, the fifteenth-century George (said to have been the abbey brewhouse) with an old coach outside, and the seventeenth-century White Hart, are reminders of the town's days as a coaching centre. Lanes leading off the High Street show good examples of thatching, with two outstanding specimens near the war memorial in the High Street itself.

EAST HENDRED

This small community on the edge of the Downs is a conservation village, rich in cruck cottages, Tudor brick and Georgian plasterwork. Racehorses are trained here and may often be seen.

In the square is Champs Chapel, now a museum. The parish church of St Augustine has a 'faceless' clock (1525) which plays a hymn every three hours, while the chapel of Hendred House (once known as the Manor of

Almshouses at Ewelme.

the Arches) is most unusual. It was started in 1256 and has been used by the Eyston family continuously since the fourteenth century, but the reformed service has never been held here. The Eystons are descendants of St Thomas More and treasure his drinking cup and a copy of the famous painting of the More family that hangs in the National Portrait Gallery.

A Shrovetide rhyme is sung at East Hendred and its singers are given a currant bun and a coin by the squire. (A similar song is sung at Brightwell-cum-Sotwell.) On the feast day of St Thomas the Apostle flour is doled out to widows and widowers of the parish.

At the western end of the village is East Hendred vineyard. The site was planted in 1972 and now exports wine, all stages of production being carried out on the premises. The more rural village of West Hendred lies between East Hendred and Ardington.

EWELME

This is one of Oxfordshire's showplaces, famous for its watercress beds, almshouses and school, and for its magnificent church (chapter 5). Jerome K. Jerome was buried in the churchyard in 1927, and Ewelme has changed little since then, despite having RAF Benson close by.

Entry to the almshouses is by the west door of the church or by the side of the school. Once there were thirteen of them, but since modernisation there are only eight. It is said

that the original thirteen were for survivors of Agincourt and fifteen Ewelme men are known to have fought there. Brick-built, the almshouses are grouped round a courtyard. On the east side the top floor contains the muniment room and part of the Master's lodging, the Master being the Regius Professor of Medicine at Oxford. Each almshouse now has running water and electricity, and there is a resident nurse. The complex was built by William de la Pole, Duke of Suffolk, and his wife Alice (Chaucer's granddaughter) in 1437.

Ewelme school is the oldest Church of England state school still to use its original building. This dates from the mid fifteenth century, with a fine timber roof. Its statutes date from 1437. The wooden doors were once the west doors of the church. Outside are coats of arms of families connected with Ewelme.

The Georgian manor house incorporates fragments of a predecessor in which Henry VIII spent his honeymoon with Catherine Howard.

EYNSHAM

Early closing Wednesday.

The small market town of Eynsham (pronounced Enshum) has been inhabited since the sixth century, as proved by the twenty sunken huts discovered at New Wintles Farm. Eynsham is approached directly from Oxford by Swinford toll bridge over the Thames. Erected by Lord Abingdon in 1769, it spans the place where, five years before, John Wesley narrowly escaped drowning. A toll is still charged for cars.

Eynsham first appears in the Anglo-Saxon Chronicle for AD 571, the next reference being in 1005 when its great Benedictine abbey was founded. This stood near the present church until its suppression in 1539.

Fourteenth-century St Leonard's has a fifteenth-century tower; inside are the remains of a wall painting of St Catherine, a century younger, possibly the work of a monk.

Acre End seems to have been the town's original nucleus, but this later shifted to the Market Place, outside the abbey gates. The ancient market cross, over 20 feet (6.1 metres) high, is supported by iron crutches. In Newland Street is an ancient thatched barn with straw birds, and in Mill Street stand the eighteenth-century vicarage and the Georgian black and white Myrtle House. Eynsham's wide selection of building materials includes stones from the demolished abbey.

FARINGDON
Early closing Thursday; market day first Thursday of the month.

Faringdon's commanding situation looking towards the Ridgeway and the Thames valley attracted the Saxons. King Edward the Elder died here in AD 924, and Domesday mentions the site of Alfred's palace as a royal manor. A weekly market was granted by King John. Faringdon was besieged by Parliament during the Civil War, but now it is a rather sleepy market town, although remaining a centre for the Vale of White Horse. Most of today's buildings are seventeenth-century or later, many built of the local limestone. The seventeenth-century town hall, built on columns, has the library on its top floor.

All Saints' church, on a hill just off the square, appears squat, having lost its spire. It is mainly Early English, with remains of a Norman predecessor. There are monuments to the Pye and Unton families, and several brasses. The beautiful south door is thirteenth-century and decorated with scrolls and dragons' heads.

Faringdon House in the Market Place was built in 1780 by Henry Pye, once Poet Laureate. It replaces the house which was held by the Royalist Sir Robert Pye and bombarded by his son, a Parliamentarian, who somehow missed!

The Folly, half a mile (800 metres) east of Faringdon, stands on a hilltop. It is a brick tower about 140 feet (43 metres) tall, constructed in 1936 by Lord Berners to give work to Faringdon's unemployed; it is now closed.

GORING
Early closing Wednesday.

This small town on the Thames has a twin village on the other side of the river in Berkshire, Streatley. Until the Edwardians exploited this lovely stretch, building their villas and boathouses, Goring was a small place with little more than church, bridge and weir. Today it is stockbroker and commuter country with a good train service to London.

The church of St Thomas of Canterbury is early twelfth-century; later in the same century an Augustinian priory was built. It was dissolved under Henry VIII, all that remains being Elvendon Priory 1½ miles (2.5 km) west. In the vestry of St Thomas's are medieval tiles, possibly from the priory. The church also has several brasses and one of England's oldest bells, cast about 1290.

Goring has eighteenth-century almshouses near the church and a seventeenth-century vicarage. The Miller of Mansfield hotel is Georgian, with a gabled seventeenth-century wing and a nineteenth-century extension.

GREAT TEW
'The place where time stood still', Great Tew has become a museum piece and been designated a conservation area. Despite its reputation for antiquity, the earliest buildings are seventeenth-century. Many are ironstone cottages, and Tew Park (1825) is a Gothic replacement of the house where Lord Falkland, Lucius Cary, entertained well known writers in the 1620s and 1630s.

The Norman St Michael's church was remodelled in the fourteenth century and owns a notable array of hatchments. The Old Forge displays costumes and craftsmen's tools.

In the 1970s the village was literally falling down, the estate then being owned by public trustees. Then the house and 4000 acre (1620 ha) estate (comprising fourteen farms and most of Great Tew itself) were bought by two businessmen and restored. They had to sell eight of the 56 houses to outsiders, as there were not enough estate workers to need them. The estate was sold in 1985 and the house and contents in 1987.

HARWELL
On the ancient Portway between Wallingford and Wantage, Harwell is known for its cherries and the Atomic Energy Research Establishment 1½ miles (2.5 km) south-west. Harwell's name derives from 'hares' well' and from here came John de Harewell, a medieval bishop of Bath and Wells.

St Matthew's church has many building styles, but a fire in 1852 badly damaged the High Street. Victorian houses largely replaced the thatched ones, but several fine cruck cottages escaped. Dating from the seventeenth century, with some fourteenth-century work, is Princes' Manor, named after the Black Prince. Edward II gave the manor of Harwell

73

to Piers Gaveston, his notorious favourite. Middle Farm (also called Bayliol's or Bronz's Manor) is part thirteenth-century; its great hall is now divided into two storeys, but basically it remains sixteenth-century work. Wellshead Farm dates partly from the fourteenth century, partly from the sixteenth, while the single-storey brick Geering Almshouses date from 1715.

HEADINGTON
Seemingly no more than a mile or two of ribbon development along the London Road, Headington originated in Roman times. It was first recorded in 1004 when there was a Saxon royal manor here and its tithes were granted to St Frideswide's Priory by Ethelred the Unready.

Today there are three Headingtons, Old, New and Quarry, each with its own High Street and parish church. In London Road are Oxford Polytechnic and the Manor, Oxford United's football ground. In Lime Walk is All Saints' church (1910, Bloomfield) and off London Road is a large teaching hospital. Between it and Old High Street is Old Headington, with its Norman church of St Andrew and The Croft, full of interesting cottages. Further along is Bury Knowle Park and off to the right is Headington Quarry, which from the fifteenth century to the nineteenth provided much of the stone for Oxford's buildings. In Quarry are stone workers' cottages and Holy Trinity church (1848/9). Headington Quarry is the home of the Headington Morris Men, and it was in Headington that Cecil Sharp first saw morris dancing (chapter 11).

Beyond Green Road roundabout is Barton Estate, to the north-east of which is Wick Farm with its Roman bath-house.

HENLEY-ON-THAMES
Early closing Wednesday; market day Thursday.
This pleasant market town is set in stockbroker country where the Chiltern Hills meet the Thames. Henley grew from a small river port into an important coaching centre and still has several old inns. Today it is known for its regattas: Henley Royal Regatta takes place during the first week of July, and the Town Regatta on the last Saturday in July or first in August.

Henley Bridge has carved faces over its central arches, representing the Thames and the Isis. Either side of the road by the bridge are the Red Lion and the Angel. The sixteenth-century Red Lion has half-timbering, some of it fake, and the Hart Street frontage is of eighteenth-century red brick. Patrons included Charles I and Prince Rupert, Boswell and Dr Johnson, the Prince Regent and

Wellington. The seventeenth-century Angel incorporates an arch from Henley's medieval bridge.

Squeezed between the Red Lion and the church is the fifteenth-century Chantry House, a timber-framed two-storey building. Its upper floor is one long aisled room, divided into bays by piers.

St Mary's church is thirteenth-century but was much restored by the Victorians. It has a monument to Lady Elizabeth Periam (1621), a sister of Sir Francis Bacon, who founded a school here for poor boys. The churchyard is bordered by almshouses founded in the 1530s and rebuilt three centuries later.

The remainder of Hart Street, as far as the Market Place, has predominantly Georgian frontages which conceal older buildings, notably the sixteenth-century Speaker's House and Old Acres, the Old Rope Walk and the Old White Hart (from the fifteenth and sixteenth centuries). The Catherine Wheel consists of a row of eighteenth-century houses.

Henley Market Place contains a variety of shop fronts, many Georgian, a sixteenth-century butcher's shop and the Queen Anne style Town Hall.

Bell Street is a busy shopping street, with the late eighteenth-century former Assembly Rooms, the fifteenth-century Bull (altered in the mid seventeenth century) and the Bear, dating from the sixteenth and seventeenth centuries. Bell Street becomes Northfield End and finishes in Georgian and neo-Georgian houses.

In New Street are an ancient timbered cottage and much Georgian construction, including one of England's oldest theatres still in use, the Kenton, opened in 1805. The Horse and Groom is timbered and sixteenth-century while Ann Boleyn Cottage and Tudor Cottage are fifteenth-century. Near Riverside are the Henley Brewery (1897), the Old Brewery House (about 1735) and the Malthouse.

LONG WITTENHAM
The Wittenham area has been inhabited since the iron age and Wittenham Clumps are a familiar local landmark.

The church was built about 1120 of Norman stone from Caen and is the third on this site. Its unusual lead font is twelfth-century and shows thirty bishops giving a blessing. The font was hidden inside wooden casing during the Civil War and so escaped being made into bullets. There are three piscinas, one very rare. It consists of a quatrefoil basin combined with the miniature effigy of a knight, only 2 feet (60 cm) long. Above him hover two angels. His armour dates from the early fourteenth century but he remains unidentified.

Long Wittenham also has St Anthony's

Well, reputed to have healing powers, a Saxon cross, the remains of a cockpit, a thirteenth-century cruck cottage, fishponds and a pigeoncote. The village holds a May Queen ceremony when children carry round a garland and distribute posies to old people. Long Wittenham is the home of the Pendon Museum (see chapter 7).

NUNEHAM COURTENAY

An early example of village planning, Nuneham lies along the A423. Apart from the Harcourt Arms and a garage, nearly all of Nuneham consists of identically designed semi-detached brick cottages, including a post office and village shop. This uniform little place resulted from the first Earl Harcourt's dislike of viewing the hovels of his tenants from his fine new mansion, Nuneham Park, in the 1760s; thus the entire peasantry was moved into suitable accommodation at a discreet distance. This removal is said to have prompted Oliver Goldsmith's *The Deserted Village* (1770).

All Saints' chapel stands in the park. Dating from 1764, it was designed by Harcourt himself. A second All Saints' (1872/4) is the village church. The house and park now belong to Oxford University and are used as a conference centre and a bookstore for the Bodleian Library. In the park are the University Arboretum and the ornate stone conduit, brought here in 1787 from Carfax in Oxford.

OXFORD

See chapters 9 and 10.

SHIPTON-UNDER-WYCHWOOD

Shipton is the largest village of the three Wychwood villages (see also Ascott-under-Wychwood). Its church was first mentioned in 1115, when it was given to Salisbury Cathedral by Henry I. The present structure is mainly twelfth-century with Norman work in the tower. There is a palimpsest brass to John and Alys Horne, reused on the reverse for their daughter-in-law, Elizabeth Thame (1548). The mid fifteenth-century font bears the Warwick emblem of the bear and ragged staff.

John Foxe wrote his *Book of Martyrs* at Shipton, and it is also one of the suggested birthplaces of William Langland, who wrote *Piers Plowman.*

The Prebendal House was probably built by Christ Church, Oxford. Of medieval origin, it was rebuilt in the seventeenth century, while the nearby tithe barn is fifteenth-century. Shipton Court, with its supposedly medieval core, was built about 1603 by the Laceys and is one of England's largest Jacobean houses. There is stained glass from about 1400, more Flemish glass, a modern chapel and a square seventeenth-century dovecote.

By the village green is the fifteenth-century Shaven Crown, so named from its former use as a guest-house for Bruern Abbey. Its impressive hall is now the hotel lounge, and Room 11, once the chapel, has a fourteenth-century fireplace. On the green is a memorial to seventeen parishioners drowned in 1874 while emigrating to New Zealand.

Milton-under-Wychwood, nearby, has a church, school and teacher's house all designed by Street in 1854. Its Queen Anne style vicarage (1898) is by Sir Thomas Jackson.

STANTON HARCOURT

See chapter 6.

SUTTON COURTENAY

A beautiful village, unspoiled even by the neighbouring cooling towers of Didcot Power Station, Sutton Courtenay stands on the Thames between Abingdon and Didcot. It is filled with trees and gardens, with timbered, stone and brick houses. A footpath leads down to a bridge and weir on the river.

Sutton Courtenay had a royal residence at Domesday; it was visited by William the Conqueror and Henry I's first child was born there. These court buildings stood between the green and the river and parts survive in the medieval manor house.

Norman Hall was built by the Courtenays in 1190 and subsequently extended, while the Abbey is a fourteenth-century house. All Saints' church dates from the twelfth century, with later work. In the churchyard are the graves of the Earl of Oxford and Asquith, prime minister from 1908 to 1916, and his wife. They built the house called The Wharf. Also buried here are the author George Orwell (Eric Blair) and Mrs Martha Pye, who died in 1822 aged 117.

THAME

Early closing Wednesday; market day Tuesday.

Pronounced 'Tame', the town grew prosperous in the 1180s and soon held a weekly market which was further developed in the thirteenth century. On the corner of Church Road are some timber-framed almshouses (1550s) and the original Lord Williams Grammar School (1569), whose pupils included John Milton, John Wilkes and John Hampden. The present school (1878) is in Oxford Road. Further along Church Road are the timber-framed brick tithe barn (sixteenth-century) and, lastly, the church of St Mary the Virgin (chapter 5).

Nearby is the beautiful Prebendal, first mentioned in 1234. Originally it had hall, solar and chapel, of which the two last remain. The Prebendal became a farmhouse with outbuildings in the early nineteenth century but was restored in 1836 when the hall became a

75

dwelling. Today it is a private residence.

In Lower High Street is Thatcher's restaurant (about 1550) and many fine brick and timber buildings.

Near the Victorian town hall, on the wall of an outfitter's shop, is a plaque commemorating John Hampden, who died in a house on this site from wounds received at the battle of Chalgrove Field in 1643. Beyond the town hall is the Bird Cage, a picturesque timber-framed inn with overhanging eaves and lattice windows. It was once a leper house, and its name is said to come from its use as a prison for French soldiers during the Napoleonic Wars. Upper High Street is one of the widest streets in Britain and lined with buildings ranging from Stuart to Victorian.

Thame Show, held on the third Thursday of September, is claimed to be the biggest one-day show in England. Thame Park, 1½ miles (2.5 km) south of the town, is on the site of the Cistercian Thame Abbey, much of which remains in the present house, now a private home.

WALLINGFORD
Early closing Wednesday; market day Friday.

Wallingford grew up in a strategic position where the Icknield Way forded the Thames. Wallingford Bridge was first mentioned in 1141; the present bridge is of thirteenth-century origin, much rebuilt in 1751 and 1809.

The squarish street pattern shows Wallingford's Saxon origins. It was the largest defended town in Wessex and had its own mint. The Conqueror allowed the citizens an hour's grace when imposing a curfew on England. Wallingford's charter was granted in 1155, 32 years before London's. Fire has destroyed much of the medieval town, most of the remaining buildings dating from the seventeenth and eighteenth centuries. Some buildings, like the Lamb Arcade and the George, have been renewed and restored.

Medieval Wallingford had eleven parishes but only three churches are left, although some of the vanished ones are remembered in street names. The oldest church, St Leonard's, has Saxon herringbone stonework. The church was badly damaged by Parliamentarian troops quartered there. Although rebuilt, it retains two Norman arches. St Peter's, now redundant, has a hollow spire rising from an octagonal lantern. Rebuilt in the eighteenth century, the church has a clock from London's Horse Guards, a gift from Oxford's first professor of English law, Sir William Blackstone, who lies here — under a black stone. St Mary's was completely rebuilt in 1854 except for its fifteenth-century tower. There is a Quaker meeting house (1724) in Castle Street. For the castle see chapter 4.

Wallingford Town Hall (1670) bears the borough coat of arms. In its upper storey is the great chamber with portraits by Lawrence and Gainsborough, the fifteenth-century town seal and a silver mace. The Corn Exchange (1856) has a fine cast iron roof; it is now used as a theatre and cinema. Flint House, in High Street, is Wallingford's museum (chapter 7).

WANTAGE
Early closing Thursday; market day Wednesday.

A Roman villa consisting of five rooms, one with a hypocaust system, was found on Chainhill Farm at Wantage. Coins found there date its occupation to between the second and fourth centuries AD.

In AD 849 King Alfred was born at Wantage, indicating that there was a royal palace there. Saxon Wantage was burnt by the Danes in 1001. The present town dates largely from the seventeenth and eighteenth centuries.

In the Market Place is a statue of Alfred by Count Gleichen. It is a smaller edition of the one at Winchester and was given to Wantage in 1877. Here too is the Bear Hotel (1635). King Alfred's Grammar School (1850) has a Norman doorway. In Newbury Street are the brick-built Stile's Almshouses (1690), the courtyard cobbled with sheeps' knuckle bones.

Once two churches occupied Wantage churchyard, but one was demolished in the mid nineteenth century. The surviving church of Saints Peter and Paul dates mainly from the thirteenth to fifteenth centuries. In the fifteenth century a chantry, now the Lady Chapel, was given by Wantage trade guilds. Much restoration was done by Street, who also added the south chancel chapel. There is a brass to Sir Ivo Fitzwarren (1412), who was supposedly the father of Dick Whittington's wife, Alice. Another Fitzwarren, Sir William, lies here with another Alice. Across from the church is the Vale and Downland Museum Centre (chapter 7).

WATLINGTON
Early closing Wednesday.

The narrow winding streets of this small town at the foot of the Chilterns are packed with old houses of all ages, although the inn where John Hampden spent the night before Chalgrove Field has disappeared. The steepled brick town hall, with the date 1665 over its arcade, once housed the grammar school. In Church Street are Elizabethan thatched cottages and there are others in Chapel Road. St Leonard's church was rebuilt in 1877 in stone and flint, leaving only its fifteenth-century tower and some ancient brasses. Watlington Castle once stood near the churchyard.

Just outside the town are the Icknield Way and the Ridgeway (chapter 2), offering good walking and picnicking opportunities. Watlington Hill, 700 feet (213 metres) high, is an area of chalk downland belonging to the National Trust (chapter 2).

WHEATLEY
Early closing Wednesday.
Wheatley was once an important Roman settlement. Parts of a large villa were excavated in the nineteenth century on Castle Hill, 1 mile (1.5 km) south-east of the church, and a Roman cemetery was discovered in the twentieth century.

Today Wheatley is largely Victorian, although it gives an impression of being older. Earlier buildings include the partly sixteenth-century Manor House and the early seventeenth-century Rectory Farm and Mulberry Court. The King's Arms bears the date 1756 on its gable.

A disused quarry, now enclosing a recreation ground, has a pyramid-shaped lock-up. Windowless and topped by a ball, it is reputed to be by Vanbrugh but was built by a local man called Cooper in 1834.

Nearby Holton Park is now a school. In the predecessor of the present Georgian house, Cromwell's daughter, Bridget, married Henry Ireton, the Parliamentary commander, in 1646.

WITNEY
Early closing Tuesday; market days Thursday and Saturday.
Witney is the chief town of west Oxfordshire and exerts considerable influence upon the surrounding villages, which traditionally depended on its blanket-making for a living.

In Oxford Road are Townesend's Almshouses (1821) and other terraced cottages, once glovemakers' and blanket workers' homes. Wood Green has fine Georgian houses and Victorian Holy Trinity church. In Bridge Street are blanket mills and Staple Hall, reputedly built by Roger de Stapledon, founder of Exeter College, Oxford.

Witney High Street has been overdeveloped and its line of old houses spoilt. On the left is Blanket Hall (1721), where blankets were checked, and in Market Square, busy with traffic, is the town hall, built with stone pillars and arches. Nearby are the Butter Cross (1660), the Angel and the Marlborough Hotel.

The broad Church Green is flanked by stone houses with courtyards and alleyways. Some houses are Victorian or Georgian like the Fleece and Oriel House, others older. The Hermitage, a plague retreat for Oxonians, is early sixteenth-century. At the end of Church Green is St Mary's (chapter 5) with almshouses built in 1724 (renewed in the 1860s). On the opposite side is Witney Grammar School (1662) and behind the church is the Leys, Witney's sports and recreation ground, where Witney Feast is held in September.

The lock-up at Wheatley.

WOODSTOCK
Early closing Wednesday.
Woodstock is a sophisticated country town astride the A34 Oxford to Stratford-upon-Avon road; it is also the site of Blenheim Palace (chapter 6). It is one of the last centres for the formerly widespread Oxfordshire glovemaking industry, Woodstock gloves having been presented to distinguished visitors for centuries.

The original manor house, which features in Scott's *Woodstock*, stood in what is now Blenheim Park, near the bridge. It was the birthplace of the Black Prince and was damaged by Cromwell. It survived into the eighteenth century, however, only to be demolished in the 1720s by order of Sarah, Duchess of Marlborough.

Woodstock's stone buildings, its solid public houses, hotels and restaurants, such as the Marlborough Arms, the Bear, the Feathers and the Dorchester, combine with its boutiques and antique shops to give it an air of age and prosperity. Old Woodstock lies on the outskirts, to the north.

In Park Street are Fletcher's House, now the County Museum (chapter 7), and Chaucer's House, said to stand on the site of a house owned by the poet's son, Thomas. St Mary Magdalen's church has a Norman south doorway, a fifteenth-century west porch and an eighteenth-century tower.

13
Tourist information centres

Abingdon: 8 Market Place, Abingdon OX14 3UD. Telephone: 0235 22711.
Banbury: Banbury Museum, 8 Horsefair, Banbury. Telephone: 0295 59855.
Burford: The Brewery, Sheep Street, Burford OX8 4LP. Telephone: 099382 3558.
Chipping Norton: 22 New Street, Chipping Norton. Telephone: 0608 41320.
Cropredy: The Wharf, Cropredy, Banbury. Telephone: 029575 8203. (Spring and summer only.)
Faringdon: The Pump House, 5 Market Place, Faringdon SN7 7HL. Telephone: 0367 22191. (Spring and summer only.)
Henley-on-Thames: Town Hall, Market Place, Henley-on-Thames RG9 2AQ. Telephone: 04391 578034.
Oxford: St Aldates Chambers, St Aldates, Oxford OX1 1DY. Telephone: 0865 726871.
Thame: Town Hall, High Street, Thame OX9 3DP. Telephone: 084421 2834.
Wallingford: 9 St Martin's Street, Wallingford OX10 0AL. Telephone: 0491 35351 extension 3810.
Witney: Cogges Farm Museum, Church Lane, Cogges, Witney OX8 6LA. Telephone: 0993 72602. (Spring and summer only.)
Witney: Town Hall, Market Square, Witney OX8 6AG. Telephone: 0993 4379.
Woodstock: The Library, Hensington Road, Woodstock OX7 1JQ. Telephone: 0993 811038.

Stanton Harcourt.

OXFORDSHIRE

* Country park, etc. (Ch. 2)
⊓ Archaeological site (Ch. 3)
C Castle (Ch. 4)
A Monastic ruin (Ch. 4)
+ Church (Ch. 5)
▲ Historic house & garden (Ch. 6)
M Museum (Ch. 7)
O Other place to visit (Ch. 8)
■ Town or village (Ch. 12)

M Claydon

Hornton
Horley
C Hanwell

M ■ BANBURY

▲ Broughton Castle

Bloxham M
■ + Adderbury

+ South Newington

C Deddington   ■ Cottisford

⊓ Rollright Stones
▲ Chastleton House   ■ Great Tew

M ■ CHIPPING NORTON
⊓ Hoar Stone
⊓ Hawk Stone

* Somerton Meads

⊓ Hoar Stone Long Barrow
▲ Rousham House

■ BICESTER

R. Evenlode
Lyneham Camp ⊓
Wychwood *

⊓ Thor Stone
+ Spelsbury

* Charlbury M

M WOODSTOCK
▲ * Blenheim
O Combe Mill
+ Bladon

R. Cherwell

R. Ray

* Otmoor

Studley ▲ Priory

Taynton
* Quarry
BURFORD
+ M R. Windrush   WITNEY
O
Widford ⊓
C Minster Lovell
O Cotswold Wildlife Park
Ducklington Meadow

Ascott-under-Wychwood
Shipton-under Wychwood

North Leigh
+ M + Cogges
+ South Leigh
Eynsham ■

M Long Hanborough
+ Yarnton
* Pixey and Yarnton Meads

MO Filkins

Stanton ▲ Harcourt Manor

A Godstow Headington
+ Binsey   Forest Hill +
■ OXFORD *
C M + O * Waterperry +
Shotover Park Wheatley
Iffley + *   Cowley

R. Thame
■ + THAME
O Rycote Chapel

+ Great Milton

+ Langford   ■ Bampton

R. Thames

Kelmscott ▲ Manor

■ Nuneham Courtenay

Chinnor + ✳ Chinnor Hill
Oakley Hill *
* Aston Rowant Nature Reserve

▲ Buscot Park

Pusey ▲ Kingston House
O House ⊓ House
Gardens ⊓ Cherbury Camp
Charney Bassett

FARINGDON
■ Hatford +
O
Great Coxwell   + Stanford-in-the-Vale

ABINGDON
M + A

Clifton Hampden

+ Dorchester-on-Thames
■ M
Milton Manor ▲ House
Sutton Courtenay
Long Wittenham
⊓ Sinodun Camp
M   ■ * Watlington

M U.ffington

M Uffington

White Horse
▲ Kingstone Lisle Park
+ Sparsholt
M
WANTAGE
⊓ Segsbury Camp
Ashdown House ▲
⊓ ⊓ ⊓
Wayland's Smithy
⊓ Uffington Castle
⊓ Alfred's Castle

East Hendred   ■ Harwell

O Ardington

O ■ DIDCOT

Benson M
■ CM
WALLINGFORD

⊓ Blewburton Hill

▲ Nuffield Place

Swyncombe Downs

+ Ewelme   Stonor ▲ Park

Wellplace Zoo
O
⊓
Devil's Ninepins

Warburg * Reserve
Maharajah's ▲ Well O
Greys Court
■ HENLEY-ON-THAMES

■ Goring

M 40

▲ Mapledurham House
R. Thames

79

Index